NEAPOLITAN
COOKING

PIZZAS AND CALZONI, SAUCES, PASTA,
FIRST COURSES, MEATS AND FISH, VEGETABLES,
FRIED FOODS, EGGS AND DESSERTS

165 FULLY ILLUSTRATED RECIPES
WITH HELPFUL HINTS AND SUGGESTIONS

BONECHI

© CASA EDITRICE BONECHI, Via Cairoli, 18 b, Florence - Italy.
Tel. +39 055576841 - Fax +39 0555000766
E-mail: bonechi@bonechi.it   Website: www.bonechi.it

Project and editorial concept: Casa Editrice Bonechi
Text: Elisabetta Piazzesi *and* Salvatore Giardinetto
Graphics and cover: Maria Rosanna Malagrinò
Make-up: Marcello Vivoli
Edited by: Patrizia Fabbri *and* Costanza Marsili Libelli
English translation: Julia Weiss

The photographs of the foods, property of the Bonechi Archives, *were taken by* Andrea Alteri, Andrea Fantauzzo, Aldo Settembre *and* Franco Tomasello.
Photograph on page 3 by Andrea Pistolesi, photographs on 4, top and left by Francesco Giannoni.
The other photographs on pages 4 and the photographs 5, property of the Bonechi Archives *were taken by* Paolo Giambone, Ferdinando Mainardi, Mario *and* Tiziana Pirone, *and* Fornass/Sparavigna.

The publishers wish to thank Messrs. Perrotta and SanFilippo, proprietors of the Villa Adelaide Restaurant in Marano di Napoli and the Nel Regno di Re Ferdinando II Restaurant, in Rome, respectively for their kind hospitality and help.

The accessories used in the photographs of some of the recipes were kindly supplied by Regalissimo di Tani Marzia & C., Florence.

Printed in Italy by Centro Stampa Editoriale Bonechi.

INTRODUCTION

*T*alking about the Campania region of Italy as a joyful and contented land merely reconfirms a conviction that has lasted through the centuries, ever since, Pliny coined the phrase, "Campania Felix" to describe this large and diversified area.

Overlooking a beautiful sea that is home to an incredible variety of fish, mollusks and crustaceans, kissed by a life-giving sun, with a climate that is mild all year long, this land has even reaped benefits from a feature that has caused incredible tragedies over the centuries. Due to the restless Mt. Vesuvius, the only active volcano in continental Europe, along with other constant and count-

less minor phenomena from bradyseisms to sulfur emissions the soil has become strong and fertile. And this, in turn, is reflected even today in the variety and abundance of the region's agricultural products.

Favored by this context, Neapolitan cuisine has suffered only from an over-abundance of choice, and has created recipes that have become traditional: fish, meat, vegetables and the most famous specialty, pasta - with a certain penchant for spaghetti, and pizza which has practically become the international symbol of Italy, not just Naples. And everything is fresh, genuine and flavorful, thanks to the custom of not combining dissimilar ingredi-

ents. This does not mean that Neapolitan cuisine is "poor", or quick. On the contrary, some of the sauces, meat dishes and macaroni-based recipes require hours of preparation and cooking. They seem to evoke the proverbially slow rhythms that were an historical peculiarity of Bourbon dominions in general and of the Kingdom of the Two Sicilies in particular. What it does mean is favoring essentially basic ingredients which by themselves, with their unmistakable flavor, and perhaps with the help of some spices or herbs that abound in the Neapolitan countryside can give a dish a distinctive character. Just think of the sunny freshness of tomatoes, the tasty fresh mozzarella cheese or how the fish of the Tyrrhenian sea and the meats from livestock raised on nearby farms emanate the most recondite and subtle flavors. And so, inimitable dishes were born, from "capitone al forno" to "saltimbocca alla sorrentina", from stuffed escarole to fried algae, from the omelet in tomato sauce to Neapolitan cannelloni, from spaghetti with octopus to "migliaccio con i ciccioli". Nor can we overlook the savory cakes, from "tortano" to "casatiello" that combine the intense, rustic flavors of Campania. Or the pizzas which by themselves are an entire chapter in Neapolitan cuisine, popular throughout the world, from the Far East to the Far West. And if pizza is the Neapolitan dish par excellence, it lacks no rivals when it comes to variety. Alongside of the traditional "margherita" and "Neapolitan" pizzas, or the typical "pizza with escarole" there are literally countless other varieties. Italian, international and even exotic recipes have transformed this disk of dough - that was the brainchild of Neapolitan cooks - into an "ideal space" where anyone can use and fulfill his imagination and satisfy all those wonderful cravings.

Then to close on a sweet note, there are the ex-

quisite desserts, from baba to "rococò", to crown the typical Neapolitan meal which traditionally consists of a first course, a second course with a vegetable, fruit and dessert.

In Naples the custom is to neglect hors d'oeuvres and antipasto, because too many preliminaries would risk delaying the encounter with the true essence of the table and its rituals.

The recipes in this book offer a significant selection of what can be considered the most typical Neapolitan dishes. It is a cuisine with a rich tradition, and that special touch of foods lovingly prepared in the home by grandmother's expert hands.

It is a cuisine with the flavor of Naples, its sun and its sea; flavors that can be taken anywhere by anyone who knows how to recreate the enchantment of its unique recipes.

CONTENTS

SAUCES

CLASSIC NEAPOLITAN
  MEAT SAUCE 65
FRESH TOMATO 69
GENOESE 64
GLASSA 65
MEAT SAUCE 67
PIZZAIOLA 69
SORRENTO
  TOMATOES 68

TOMATO
  CONCENTRATE 68
TOMATO STRIPS 67

DOUGH

BREAD DOUGH 73
LIGHT SHORT
  PASTRY 72

PLAIN PASTRY 73
SHORT PASTRY 72

SOUPS AND BROTHS

BEAN SOUP 84
CHICORY AND ESCAROLE SOUP 76
CLAM SAUTÉ 82
DRIED CODFISH SOUP 89
FISH SOUP 88
GREEN BEAN AND TOMATO SOUP 76
HEARTY SOUP 86
LENTIL SOUP 77
"MARITATA" SOUP 78
RED MUSSEL SOUP 84
RICE AND CABBAGE SOUP 80
SPULLECRIELLI SOUP 88
ZUCCHINI AND TOMATO SOUP 82

PASTA DISHES

FISH AND SEAFOOD

ANCHOVIES IN TORTIERA 134
BATTER FRIED WHITEBAIT 138
CALAMARY
  AND POTATOES 141
EEL ALLA MARINARA 137
FRIED EEL 138
MULLET ALLA PESCATORA 142
MULLET BAKED IN FOIL 143
OCTOPUS ALLA LUCIANA 140
OVEN-BAKED EEL 137

SEA BASS ALL'ACQUA
  PAZZA 139

STEWED CODFISH 135
STUFFED SQUID 136

MEATS

CHICKEN
  ALLA SCARPARIELLO 152
CUTLETS IN MEAT SAUCE 147
LAMB FRICASSEE 146
LEG OF LAMB
  ALLA LISETTA 149
MEAT ALLA PIZZAIOLA 150

MEAT LOAF 152
MEAT PATTIES IN TOMATO
  SAUCE 151
NEAPOLITAN KID 150
PORK RIND CUTLETS
PORK WITH PICKLED
  PEPPERS 151

RABBIT ISCHIA STYLE 150
ROLLED SHOULDER
  OF VEAL 148
SALTIMBOCCA ALLA
  SORRENTINA

VEGETABLES

CAPONATA 156
EGGPLANT BOATS 161
HEARTY SALAD 158
SAUTÉED PEPPERS
  WITH TOMATO 161
SAUTÉED TURNIP TOPS 157

STUFFED EGGPLANT 159
STUFFED ESCAROLE 162
STUFFED PEPPERS 160
ZUCCHINI ALLA SCAPECE 163

FRIED FOODS

EGGS

DESSERTS

HELPFUL HINTS

Neapolitan cuisine gets its traditional features of originality, freshness and genuinity from many typical ingredients and a few little tricks. For example herbs and spices such as **garlic** used raw, boiled, minced, pressed or sautéed in olive oil and parsley; **hot peppers** be they red or green, fresh, in oil, or dried that have displaced **pepper** with the full approval of many doctors.

Then there are the **olives**, especially the tasty variety from Gaeta which, in Naples, are often used with **capers** especially the tiny little salted ones from the island of Pantelleria that should be added to sauces just before serving because otherwise they will lose some of their wonderful flavor.

Onions are irreplaceable in many dishes; **green onions** are used in salads or make an excellent dish when cooked.

Basil is the king of the herbs. With their fresh, summery taste whole leaves are used raw, making a fine complement to tomatoes.

Celery stalks, preferably white, are essential when making broth and cooking certain vegeta-bles, and, of course, are excellent in salads.

Parsley is a basic ingredient in most fish dishes, either cooked or chopped raw, to flavor and garnish. Along with onion, carrot and celery it comprises the Neapolitan equivalent of the French bouquet garni.

Typical Neapolitan dishes also use **bay** leaves to flavor roast meats and some fish dishes such as capitone al forno. **Mint** leaves are used fresh and in small quantities in salads and some special dishes such as "scapace".

Oregano with its distinctive flavor is indispensable for dishes "alla pizzaiola".

Then there are **pine nuts** and **raisins** which are used in many stuffings and sauces. To get the best from the raisins soak them in water for at least one hour.

As to special little tricks, secrets of Neapolitan chefs, can be useful.

Pasta, especially if it is **long** and thin, like **spaghetti** should slide on the palate. To get these results, add two tablespoons of olive oil to the cooking water, lift the cooked pasta out of the water with a fork instead of draining it, and dress it quickly, preferably in individual plates rather than in a large serving bowl where the condiments tend to collect at the bottom. **Thick** and **short** pasta should be cooked in lots of salted water. When it comes to **meats**, **veal** is generally prepared in plain sauces while **beef** and **pork** are cooked in meat-based, red sauces.

Cervellatine, long, thin sausages made of ground pork in lambgut are typical of Neapolitan cuisine. Cervellatine are served as a main dish and also lend an excellent flavor to roasts. **Fish** is the king of Neapolitan cooking; when it is roasted in the oven you must cut it along the back, after you have removed the scales, cleaned and washed it. The oven should be kept at a constant 180°C/350°F , and to keep the fish tender, baste it now and then with its own juices.

As to **seafood**, boil it before you start. Soak **clams** in fresh water for 4 to 5 hours to eliminate the sand. Mussels have to be cleaned of incrustations and rinsed repeatedly until the water is perfectly clean. When you put them in a pot without water and turn on the stove they will open and release all the sea water inside.

The best **octopus** are the ones from the **rocky coasts** and that have two rows of suckers on the tentacles. Clean them carefully, first remove the insides - by turning the octopus inside out like a glove - then the eyes and beak. It is advisable to put the cleaned octo-

pus into the freezer for a few days as this tenderizes it. Then cook it whole, and remember to put a cork into the water. The cork (incredible but true!) will make the octopus more tender. Slice the octopus when it is cooked.

As to **vegetables** not many people know **friarielli** (turnip tops) a variety of broccoli from the Neapolitan countryside, and yet their tender, slightly bitter tips are the protagonists in many tasty Neapolitan dishes. It is always best to cook the other, more usual **legumes** in covered earthenware pots. Boil them slowly in a little water. It is best to add water while cooking if you realize that they are getting dry. And finally, there is **pizza** which is actually nothing more than a brilliant blend of flour, yeast, water and imagination. It is so simple, and even though purists would have them baking in wood-burning ovens, you can make excellent pizzas in your own kitchen. The main thing is to make a good dough, that should rise properly and be rolled out the right way, that is why the chapter on pizza has a special introduction of its own.

And now, as they say in Naples, and all of Italy, "Buon appetito".

IMPORTANT: UNLESS OTHERWISE SPECIFIED, ALL THE RECIPES IN THIS BOOK ARE FOR **FOUR** SERVINGS.

IN THE TEXT OF THE NAMES OF THE FOODS HAVE BEEN TRANSLATED INTO ENGLISH, WITH THE ORIGINAL ITALIAN ON THE SAME PAGE. A FEW OF THE SPECIALTIES ARE SIMPLY UNTRANSLATABLE, THEY WOULD SEEM SILLY IN ANYTHING BUT THE ORIGINAL NEAPOLITAN DIALECT. THE RECIPES ARE GIVEN IN METRIC AND IMPERIAL MEASURES, THAT IS GRAMS (**G**), OUNCES (**OZ**), KILOGRAMS (**KG**) AND POUNDS (**LB**). LIQUID MEASURES ARE METRIC, THAT IS LITERS AND FRACTIONS, AND IMPERIAL, QUARTS, PINTS AND CUPS. THE TABLESPOON IS A CLASSIC UNIT IN NEAPOLITAN COOKING AND IS UNIVERSAL.

THESE RECIPES ALL ORIGINATED IN METRIC UNITS AND CONVERSIONS CAN ALWAYS BE A PROBLEM.

HERE THE QUANTITIES HAVE BEEN ROUNDED UP OR DOWN ACCORDING TO COMMON SENSE AND CONVENIENCE, FOR EXAMPLE, 8 OUNCES ARE 225 GRAMS, 200 GRAMS HAVE BEEN CONVERTED AS 8 OUNCES, AS HAVE 250 GRAMS, DEPENDING ON THE INGREDIENTS; 500 GRAMS OF FLOUR IS ACTUALLY A LITTLE MORE THAN ONE POUND, BUT THERE IS NO SUBSTANTIAL DIFFERENCE.

OVEN TEMPERATURES ARE GIVEN IN BOTH CELSIUS AND FAHRENHEIT.

SALT AND **PEPPER** ARE PART OF NEARLY EVERY RECIPE, SO THEY ARE NOT LISTED AMONG THE INGREDIENTS.

PIZZAS AND CALZONI

MIXING AND LEAVENING

1 Place the ingredients on your work table: use all purpose flour in a mound with a little salt (in the picture, going counterclockwise: brewer's yeast, dried activated yeast), oil and water.

For 4 servings use 500 g/1 lb. flour, or use a few tablespoons less if you prefer a thin crust, 4-5 tablespoons of olive oil and 1 glass of water.

2 If you use dry, activated yeast you must mix it in with the flour (one packet of yeast is sufficient for 500 g/1 lb. of flour). This yeast works fast, and your dough will rise in about one hour.

Important: the recipes in this book are based on dry activated yeast.

3 Both fresh (about 20-25 g/1 oz) and granulated (about 10 g/$^1/_2$ oz) brewer's yeast have to be dissolved in lukewarm water (25-30°C/ 77-86°F).

Pour the dissolved yeast into the middle of the flour and combine thoroughly (leavening time is about 2 hours). After you add the yeast, let the flour rest for 5-10 minutes. If you add other ingredients, let the mixture rise for an extra half hour.

4 Add the water (if you use brewer's yeast you will not need much more water) a little at a time, kneading until it is entirely absorbed.

Add the oil, one tablespoon at a time. Knead the dough until it is soft and elastic (about 15 minutes).

Shape it into a ball, cover it with a damp cloth and let it rise.

KNEADING AND ROLLING

5 Roll out the dough with a rolling pin (or use a pasta machine) to the desired thickness. You can make one big pizza or smaller, individual pizzas. Naturally, the smaller pizzas will be thinner and crisper. The large pizza will be thicker and softer.

The ideal thickness for individual pizzas is from 5 mm to 1 cm (1/4 to 1/2 inch); large pizzas should range from 1 to 2 cm (1/2 to 1 inch).

As you can see, our recipes cover both versions, according to the topping you choose, but you can change at will. Calzoni, naturally require individual pizzas.

6 Let the dough rest a bit. If the recipe calls for it, spread the tomato purée (or fresh, chopped tomatoes), puncture the dough with a fork (this is important for thick pizzas).

If you do not have a wood-burning brick oven, place the dough in a flat pan or on oven-paper on the rack. Bake the pizza for about 20 minutes at 200-220°C (400-425°F).

As you will see, there are pizzas such as the classic Neapolitan, margherita, etc. that are baked with all the topping; others must be baked for about 10 or 15 minutes, removed from the oven, topped and then put back in for another 10 minutes or so.

To make dough for pizzas and calzoni bakers use sourdough. It takes longer and leavening time is longer, but the dough is tastier. 100 g/ 4 oz of sourdough are sufficient for 350 g /12 oz flour. Add 80 cc /3 fl. oz water to the sourdough, and knead it for 20 minutes gradually adding 150 g./6 oz. flour, salt and 1 tablespoon olive oil. Shape the dough into a ball, cover it with a cloth and let it rise for 5 to 6 hours. Roll out the dough, adding another 80 cc/3 fl oz water and 200 g/8 oz flour, 1 tablespoon olive oil and salt.

Knead for another 10 minutes, and then let the dough rest for 4 hours. Knead again, roll out and shape into a disk and let it rest for 20 minutes.

Important note: These recipes actually call for "mozzarella di bufala". Since this delicious variety is hard to come by outside of Italy, we suggest that you use any fresh mozzarella that sits in liquid. If this is not available, the next best solution is prepackaged mozzarella that can be found at most dairy counters.

1 - MARGHERITA

DOUGH:

SEE PAGE 16, ITEM 1

TOPPING:

300 G/12 OZ TOMATO PURÉE

250 G/8 OZ FRESH
    MOZZARELLA CHEESE

BASIL

OLIVE OIL

This is the queen of pizzas and not only, as almost everyone knows, because it was named after a queen of Italy, but because it is the most popular all over the world.

Prepare the dough and let it rise for one hour. Roll it out and divide it into 4 disks, generously spread the tomato purée, and top with sliced mozzarella cheese.
Salt lightly and bake in a preheated oven at 200°C/390°F for 20 minutes. Garnish with fresh basil and a squiggle of olive oil just before serving.

- *The Margherita is also excellent when made with fresh tomatoes, as you can see on the left. While the dough is rising clean 3-4 ripe tomatoes and cut them into strips. Roll out the dough, and cover the disk with slices of mozzarella (you will need a little more cheese than when you are using tomato purée), top the cheese with the fresh tomato, add a pinch of salt. Bake the pizza for 20 minutes at 200°C/390°F .*

- *The Margherita originates from the Neapolitan pizza minus the anchovies and capers. The original Neapolitan pizza was not as rich, it was more like the Marinara pizza, that is tasty and easy to prepare. Spread a generous amount of tomato purée over the disk, thinly slice a clove of garlic and scatter the slices over the pizza and add a pinch of salt. Bake for 15 minutes at 220°C/425°F. You can serve it plain, as shown, or add a few fresh basil leaves and a squiggle of olive oil.*

2 - QUATTRO STAGIONI
FOUR SEASON

Prepare the dough and let it rise for 1 hour. Clean and slice the tomatoes and the pepper.

Clean and slice the mushrooms. Sauté them in olive oil with garlic and parsley for 5 minutes; set aside and keep warm.

Roll out the dough and make 4 disks; spread the tomato purée over them and distribute the topping in wedges as follows: on the first a layer of ricotta; on the second slices of mozzarella and tomato slices; on the third the strips of pepper and on the fourth the remaining tomato.

Salt lightly and bake at 220°C/425°F for 15 minutes.

Remove the pizzas from the oven and put the mushrooms over the peppers, the clams, mussels and shrimp on the tomato, the ham cut into little pieces on the ricotta. Bake for another 5 minutes, then garnish with olives and basil right before serving.

DOUGH:

SEE PAGE 16, ITEM 1

TOPPING:

250 G/8 OZ TOMATO PURÉE

2-3 RIPE TOMATOES

4 STRIPS OF RED BELL PEPPER

250 G/8 OZ FRESH MOZZARELLA CHEESE

200 G/8 OZ RICOTTA CHEESE

200 G/8 OZ MUSHROOMS

100G SHELLED SHRIMP

4 SLICES CURED HAM

LEMON JUICE

PARSLEY

1 CLOVE GARLIC

400 G/ 14 OZ CLAMS AND MUSSELS

BLACK OLIVES AND BASIL

OLIVE OIL

3 - FAMILIARE
FAMILY

DOUGH:

SEE PAGE 16, ITEM 1

TOPPING:

250 G/8 OZ FRESH MOZZARELLA
    CHEESE

A HEAD OF ENDIVE

PITTED BLACK OLIVES

CAPERS

OREGANO

OLIVE OIL

Prepare the dough and let it rise for 1 hour. Clean the endive, toss it into boiling water for 5 minutes; drain and chop. Roll out the dough and divide into four disks. Cut the mozzarella into little pieces and sprinkle generously over the dough, season with salt and olive oil. Bake at 200°C/390°F for 10 minutes.

• Do you like salad? If you do, there is a pizza with chicory. Clean a nice head of chicory and separate the leaves, and select the most tender ones. Cover the pizzas with mozzarella, salt and olive oil. Bake at 200°C/390°F for 20 minutes. Remove from the oven and arrange the chicory leaves on top of the pizza and sprinkle with flakes of Parmesan cheese (see picture on the left).

4 - CURIOSA
CURIOUS

DOUGH:

SEE PAGE 16, ITEM 1

TOPPING:

250 G/8 OZ FRESH MOZZARELLA
   CHEESE

3-4 BUNCHES OF RUCOLA

700 G/1 $^3/_4$ LB SHELLED
   SHRIMP

FLAKED PARMESAN CHEESE

OLIVE OIL

Prepare the dough and let it rise for 1 hour. Clean the rucola and chop it up. Roll out the dough and divide it into 4 disks. Chop up the mozzarella and cover the disks with it, add a pinch of salt and a squiggle of olive oil. Bake the pizzas at 200°C/390°F for 10 minutes.
Remove them from the oven, top with the rucola and shrimp, bake for another 15 minutes. Sprinkle with flaked parmesan cheese right before serving.

• *Rucola also goes very well with speck (you will need 4 slices). Cover the pizzas with mozzarella, tear up the speck and place the pieces over the cheese. Bake at 200°C/390°F for 20 minutes. Remove the pizzas from the oven, sprinkle with the rucola and flaked parmesan cheese and serve (see illustration on the right).*

5 - MOSAIC

DOUGH:

SEE PAGE 16, ITEM 1

TOPPING:

2-3 RIPE TOMATOES

150 G/6 OZ FONTINA CHEESE
(1 THICK SLICE)

700 G/1 ³/₄ LB MIXED
VEGETABLES IN OLIVE OIL
WELL-DRAINED (1 JAR)

PARSLEY

OLIVE OIL

Prepare the dough and let it rise for 1 hour. Clean the tomatoes. Roll out a thick disk of dough; cover it with the sliced tomatoes, strips of Fontina cheese, add a squiggle of olive oil and pinch of salt. Bake at 220°C/425°F for 15 minutes. Remove the pizza from the oven, add the drained vegetables and bake for another 5 minutes.

Remove from the oven, sprinkle with chopped parsley, and serve.

• *Pizza is a wonderful vehicle for recycling leftovers, such as cooked spaghetti in tomato sauce. Roll out the dough, cover it with mozzarella cheese and then add the spaghetti.*
Garnish with capers, oregano, salt and a little olive oil.
Bake at 200°C/390°F for 20 minutes, top with parmesan cheese and chopped parsley as shown.

6 - MEDITERRANEO
MEDITERRANEAN

DOUGH:

SEE PAGE 16, ITEM 1

TOPPING:

250 G/8 OZ CRUSHED PEELED
   TOMATOES (CANNED),

250 G/8 OZ FRESH MOZZARELLA
   CHEESE

BLACK OLIVES, PITTED

CAPERS IN VINEGAR

BASIL

OLIVE OIL SEASONED WITH HOT
   PEPPERS

Prepare the dough and let it rise for 1 hour. Roll out the dough and divide it into 4 disks. Spread a thin layer of crushed peeled tomatoes (canned) on each disk, top with the mozzarella cheese, a generous amount of olives, a sprinkling of capers and a pinch of salt. Bake at 200°C/390°F for 20 minutes.
Garnish with fresh basil leaves and a squiggle of the spicy olive oil.

For a very tasty variation of this pizza, add anchovy fillets, thinly slicked onion and a few thin slices of garlic.

7 - SCOGLIO
SEAFOOD

DOUGH:

SEE PAGE 16, ITEM 1

TOPPING:

700 G/1 ³/₄ LB CHERRY
    TOMATOES

250 G/8 OZ MOZZARELLA
    CHEESE

450 G/1 LB CUTTLEFISH
    OR SQUID

500 G/1 LB MUSSELS
    OR CLAMS

500 G/1 LB SCAMPI OR GIANT
    SHRIMP

2 CLOVES GARLIC

PARSLEY

DRIED RED HOT PEPPERS

DRY WHITE WINE

OLIVE OIL

Prepare the dough and let it rise for 1 hour. Place the mollusks in a pan, add the wine, pepper, garlic and parsley and steam them open. Remove the shells, chop the clams and mussels, cook covered with 3-4 tablespoons of olive oil, garlic, parsley, salt, red hot peppers and a splash of white wine for 15 minutes.

Quickly scald the shellfish in a little salted water.

Roll out the dough and divide it into 4 disks. Cover the disks with the mozzarella cheese, the mollusks and shellfish.

Bake at 200°C/390°F for 20 minutes.

• *Pizza and the sea, an unbeatable duo. Top the pizzas with mozzarella cheese, sliced tomato, black olives and 5-6 anchovy fillets per person. Garnish with oregano and olive oil. Bake at 220°C/425°F for 20 minutes, serve hot and steaming as shown.*

8 - TONNO E CIPOLLA
TUNA FISH AND ONION

DOUGH:

SEE PAGE 16, ITEM 1

TOPPING:

250 G/8 OZ CRUSHED PEELED
    TOMATOES (CANNED),

250 G/8 OZ FRESH MOZZARELLA
    CHEESE

250 G/8 OZ TUNA FISH, OIL
    PACK

1-2 GOLDEN ONIONS

PITTED BLACK OLIVES

PARSLEY, CHOPPED

OLIVE OIL

Prepare the dough and let it rise for 1 hour. Peel and slice the onions, and put them in cold water to soak for 15 minutes (this makes them taste milder), drain and dry.

Roll out the dough and divide it into 4 disks. Sprinkle crumbled mozzarella cheese, the sliced onion and a handful of olives onto each one; add a pinch of salt.

Bake at 220°C/425°F for 10 minutes; remove from the oven and top with the crumbled tuna fish; bake for another 10 minutes. Add a squiggle of olive oil and a sprinkling of freshly chopped parsley.

There is a variation on this pizza that uses scallions or pickled (in vinegar) baby onions, both of which go excellently with tuna. Creamy cheeses such as robiola or crescenza are excellent with tuna garnished with green olives.

9 - FANTASTICA
FANTASTIC

DOUGH:

SEE PAGE 16, ITEM 1

TOPPING:

250 G/8 OZ CRUSHED PEELED
  TOMATOES (CANNED)

250 G/8 OZ FRESH
  MOZZARELLA CHEESE

200 G/8 OZ SMOKED
  PROVOLONE CHEESE

150 G/6 OZ FRESH PECORINO
  CHEESE

AGED PECORINO CHEESE
  GRATED

2-3 SAUSAGES OR PEPPERONI

4 SLICES HAM.

300 G/12 OZ SPINACH

200 G/8 OZ MUSHROOMS

1 CLOVE GARLIC

OLIVE OIL

Prepare the dough and let it rise for 1 hour. Clean the spinach, cook in lightly salted boiling water, drain, squeeze out the excess water and chop.

Wash the mushrooms and sauté in a skillet with 2 or 3 tablespoons olive oil, garlic, salt and pepper. Roll out the dough and divide it into 4 disks. Spread a thin layer of crushed peeled tomatoes. Top in sections: mozzarella with the ham and mushrooms; spinach with the crumbled sausage (or pepperoni slices), and crumbled smoked provolone and fresh pecorino.

Bake at 220°C/425°F for 20 minutes. Sprinkle the grated, aged pecorino cheese onto the pizzas right before serving.

27

10 - PROSCIUTTO E FONTINA
HAM AND FONTINA CHEESE

DOUGH:

SEE PAGE 16, ITEM 1

TOPPING:

450 G/1 LB MOZZARELLA

2-3 SLICES FONTINA CHEESE

4 SLICES CURED HAM

60 G/2 OZ BUTTER

Prepare the dough and let it rise for 1 hour. Roll out the dough and divide it into 4 disks. Sprinkle crumbled mozzarella over each one, top with half a slice of Fontina, a pat of butter, one slice of ham, torn into pieces, a pinch of salt and dash of pepper.
Bake at 220°C/425°F for 20 minutes and serve hot. A traditional alternative is to garnish the pizza with slices of ripe tomato.

On the subject of "white" pizzas, that is pizza without tomato topping, there is a delicious version topped with emmenthal and similar cheeses. After you have spread the cheeses, garnish with a squiggle of olive oil, salt and pepper (for an added touch of flavor, sprinkle some chopped shallots on top); bake at 220°C/425°F for 10 minutes. Remove from the oven, sprinkle flaked cheese and bacon (or speck) on the top; bake for another 5 minutes.

11 - BISMARCK

DOUGH:

SEE PAGE 16, ITEM 1

TOPPING:

250 G/8 OZ CRUSHED PEELED
  TOMATOES

250 G/8 OZ FRESH MOZZARELLA
  CHEESE

4 EGGS

BASIL

Prepare the dough and let it rise for 1 hour. Roll out the dough and divide it into 4 disks. Spread the tomato over each, and add a pinch of salt. Cut the mozzarella into chunks and distribute it over the pizzas, then break an egg in the center of each pizza.
Bake at 220°C/425°F for 20 minutes, garnish with fresh basil leaves and serve.
If you prefer slightly undercooked eggs, bake the pizza for 10 minutes, remove from the oven, add the egg then bake for the remaining 10 minutes.

- *Here is a happy alternative for people who just don't like eggs. Clean 250 g/8 oz. mushrooms, sauté them lightly in a skillet with 2-3 tablespoons of olive oil, one clove crushed garlic, chopped parsley, salt and pepper. Prepare the pizzas with the tomato and mozzarella, top with the mushrooms.*
Bake at 200°C/390°F for 20 minutes, garnish with basil leaves as shown just before serving.

29

12 - PRIMAVERA
SPRINGTIME

DOUGH:

SEE PAGE 16, ITEM 1

TOPPING:

250 G/8 OZ CRUSHED PEELED
    TOMATOES (CANNED)

200 G/8 OZ FRESH, SOFT
    CHEESE

HEART OF CELERY

1 TENDER CARROT

1 ZUCCHINI

1 FENNEL

1 TENDER ARTICHOKE

FRESH OLIVE OIL

Prepare the dough and let it rise for 1 hour. While the dough is rising clean the vegetables and slice them *à la julienne*. Roll out the dough until it is 1,5 to 2 (inch) cm thick and spread the crushed peeled tomatoes; add the soft, fresh cheese, a generous squiggle of olive oil and a pinch of salt.
Bake at 220°C/425°F for 20 minutes.

Remove from the oven and while the pizza is still hot and smoking, cover it with the *julienne* of vegetables, add some more olive oil, a generous dash of pepper and serve.

If you like, you can use mozzarella cheese; if you like a spicy pizza, try olive oil seasoned with hot peppers.

13 - GRUYÈRE E INDIVIA BELGA

GRUYERE AND ENDIVE

DOUGH:

SEE PAGE 16, ITEM 1

TOPPING:

250 G/8 OZ CRUSHED PEELED TOMATOES (CANNED)

3-5 HEADS OF ENDIVE LETTUCE

300 G/12 OZ GRUYERE CHEESE, THINLY SLICED

GRATED PARMESAN CHEESE

OREGANO

Prepare the dough and let it rise for 1 hour. While the dough is rising, cook the whole heads of endive for 5 minutes in slightly salted boiling water so that they remain closed. Drain and dry thoroughly. When they have cooled, slice each head lengthwise. Roll out the dough (about 5-6 mm - ¼ inch) and divide it into 4 disks.

Spread the crushed peeled tomatoes over each disk, add a pinch of salt. Top with the gruyere slices.

Bake at 200°C/390°F for 10 minutes. Arrange the endive leaves like petals, bake for another 10 minutes; sprinkle with grated parmesan cheese and serve.

14 - ORTOLANA
VEGETARIAN

DOUGH:

SEE PAGE 16, ITEM 1

BREWER'S YEAST

SPINACH

TOPPING:

4-5 RIPE TOMATOES

4 ANCHOVIES

SEMI-AGED PECORINO CHEESE

Wash the spinach, then scald in lightly salted water. Drain, squeeze out the excess water and then purée it in the blender.
Place the flour on your work table, add the brewer's yeast dissolved in water and a small handful of the spinach purée. Combine, and knead the mixture, gradually adding all the spinach and the olive oil, drop by drop. Let the dough rise for 90 minutes. Wash the anchovies thoroughly under cold, running water, remove the bones and cut them into strips. Clean and slice the tomatoes, then cut each slice in half.
Roll out the dough and top with the sliced tomato, the anchovies and some of the flaked pecorino cheese.
Bake at 220°C/425°F for 20 minutes.

Instead of spinach you can also use savoy cabbage for tasty and colorful results.

15 - GENEROSA
GENEROUS

DOUGH:

SEE PAGE 16, ITEM 1

TOPPING:

500 G/1 LB ASPARAGUS

500 G/1 LB MUSSELS

4 RIPE TOMATOES

250 G/8 OZ FRESH MOZZARELLA
   CHEESE

1 CLOVE GARLIC

PARSLEY

ESTRAGON (OPTIONAL)

30 G/1 OZ BUTTER

OLIVE OIL

Prepare the dough and let it rise for 1 hour. Tie the asparagus into a bunch; place the bunch upright in a deep pot and add water until the white part of the stems is covered.
Boil, covered for 15 minutes, drain and dry. Cut off the tough, bottom part of the stems, and sauté the rest in a skillet with melted butter and a pinch of salt and pepper.
Clean the tomatoes; slice 2 of them and finely chop the other two, season with olive oil and salt.
Clean the mussels and steam them open in a pan with a little water, 1 clove garlic and a sprig of parsley. Remove the shells and keep the mussels warm. Roll out the dough, it should be thick and top it with the chopped tomatoes. Arrange the asparagus, the sliced tomatoes and sliced mozzarella cheese and garnish with the mussels. Bake at 200°C/390°F for 20 minutes, garnish with estragon, if you like and slice the pizza at the table.

16 - AFFUMICATA
SMOKED

DOUGH:

SEE PAGE 16, ITEM 1

TOPPING:

4-5 RIPE TOMATOES

250 G/8 OZ FRESH MOZZARELLA
    CHEESE

300 G/12 OZ SMOKED
    PROVOLONE CHEESE

GRATED PARMESAN CHEESE
(OPTIONAL)

OLIVE OIL

Prepare the dough and let it rise for 1 hour.
Wash the tomatoes, cut them open and remove the seeds; then make nice even slices. Remove the outer skin from the provolone and cut it into cubes.
Roll out the dough and divide it into 4 disks. Pour a squiggle of olive oil onto each one, then top with crumbled mozzarella cheese, the cubed provolone and the tomato slices.
Bake at 200°C/390°F for 20 minutes. Serve hot - sprinkle with grated parmesan if you like.

A smoky flavor is fine on pizza, and even better - in our opinion - on calzoni. Just take a whiff of the fragrant cloud that emanates from a piping hot calzone filled with bacon or speck. You can enhance the flavor if you add ingredients to the filling such as red radicchio and sautéed mushrooms or potatoes and eggs.

17 - PASTORELLA
SHEPHERDESS

DOUGH:

SEE PAGE 16, ITEM 1

TOPPING:

250 G/8 OZ FRESH MOZZARELLA CHEESE

200 G/7 OZ FRESH RICOTTA CHEESE

150 G/6 OZ PEPPERONI SAUSAGE

BASIL

OLIVE OIL

Prepare the dough and let it rise for 1 hour. Put the ricotta cheese into a mixing bowl and blend it with a fork, adding 2 tablespoons of olive oil, a pinch of salt and a dash of pepper; blend until smooth and creamy.

Roll out the dough to a thickness of about 5-6 mm - ¼ inch and divide it into 4 disks, top with crumbled mozzarella cheese.

Spoon the ricotta mixture onto the mozzarella and then arrange the pepperoni sausage cut into strips. Bake at 220°C/425°F for 20 minutes. Garnish with fresh basil leaves and serve hot.

Another "rustic" and spicy idea? Sauté radicchio trevigiano, or spinach or endive leaves in olive oil, garlic and hot peppers.

Bake the pizza at 200°C/390°F for 10 minutes, arrange the vegetables on the pizza and top with slices of smoked scamorza cheese or spicy provolone, bake for another 10 minutes.

This combination of flavors is also ideal for calzoni fillings.

18 - RUSTICANA

DOUGH:

SEE PAGE 16, ITEM 1

TOPPING:

400 G /14 OZ CRUSHED PEELED
   TOMATOES (CANNED)

450 G/1LB FRESH MOZZARELLA
   CHEESE

150 G/6 OZ MILD PROVOLONE
   CHEESE

200 G/8 OZ HAM
   (1 THICK SLICE)

7-8 ARTICHOKE HEARTS
   IN OLIVE OIL

PITTED BLACK OLIVES

BASIL

OLIVE OIL

Prepare the dough and let it rise for 1 hour. Cut the ham and provolone cheese into cubes; crumble half the mozzarella, slice the other half. Roll out the dough and divide it into 4 disks, but cut off enough dough to use for trimming. Top with the tomatoes, sprinkle the crumbled mozzarella over the tomatoes, and add a pinch of salt.

Cut the dough you set aside into strips, and put two strips on each pizza to "divide" it into quarters.

Working clockwise, top each quarter as follows: cubed ham; cubed provolone; sliced mozzarella; artichoke hearts. Garnish with the olives and basil leaves.

Bake at 220°C/425°F for 20 minutes.

• *Another "homey" idea? While the dough is rising cut an eggplant into thin, lengthwise slices, cover the slices with coarse salt and let them stand for 20 minutes. Rinse the slices and then cook them over the grill (5-6 minutes on each side), and brush them with olive oil flavored with 2 cloves of garlic. Top the pizza with mozzarella cheese, arrange the eggplant slices as shown, add a pinch of salt and then bake at 220°C/425°F for 20 minutes.*

36

• *Rustic is as rustic does - here is an idea for an after-school snack, the easy pizza shown here on the right. Roll out the dough thickly and place it in a round, flat oven pan, top with slice tomato, garlic cloves, salt, pepper and olive oil. Bake at 220°C/425°F for 20 minutes and serve piping hot.*

19 - STRAPAZZATA
SCRAMBLED

DOUGH:

SEE PAGE 16, ITEM 1

TOPPING:

400 G/14 OZ SPINACH

4 EGGS

200 G/8 OZ GORGONZOLA
    CHEESE

HONEY

30 G/1 OZ BUTTER

OLIVE OIL

Prepare the dough and let it rise for 1 hour. Wash the spinach under running water and boil in a little salted water. Drain and squeeze out the excess water, chop and season with a little olive oil.

Melt a pat of butter in a hot skillet, scramble the eggs and season with a little salt, then set aside and keep warm.

Roll out the dough to a thickness of about 1.5 cm ($^3/_4$ inch) and place it in a round, flat oven pan, top with the chopped spinach and scrambled eggs.

Arrange slices of gorgonzola cheese to form spokes as shown, and then bake at 220°C/425°F for 20 minutes.

Serve hot with a tablespoon of honey, an unusual and elegant touch for this refined combination of flavors.

If you like your eggs soft, first bake the spinach-covered dough for 10 minutes, remove from the oven and add the eggs and cheese, and bake for the last 10 minutes.

A slightly more elaborate version? Make a pretty omelet that you can flavor with herbs such as dill, basil, estragon, marjoram, etc., cut it into slices and arrange them neatly on the dough.

20 - MONGIBELLO
MT. ETNA

DOUGH:

SEE PAGE 16, ITEM 1

TOMATO CONCENTRATE

GROUND RED HOT PEPPERS

TOPPING:

3 SLICES CURED HAM

250 G/8 OZ FRESH MOZZARELLA
CHEESE

2 BUNCHES OF RUCOLA

1 BUNCH CHERRY TOMATOES

50 G/2 OZ SOYBEAN SPROUTS,

OLIVE OIL FLAVORED WITH HOT
PEPPERS

After you have combined the flour and yeast, dissolve 2 tablespoons of tomato concentrate in a glass of lukewarm water, add it to the mixture along with $^1/_2$ teaspoon of ground red hot peppers. Add the oil and knead until all the ingredients are fully blended; make a ball of dough, cover it with a cloth and let it rise for 90 minutes.

While the dough is rising clean the rucola and the soybean sprouts; chop the rucola.

Cut the ham into thin strips and sauté it quickly in a skillet with a drop of olive oil; remove the strips from the skillet and drain them on a paper towel.

Roll out the dough and top it with the rucola, the mozzarella cheese cut into pieces and the tomatoes, season with a pinch of salt and the olive oil flavored with hot peppers.

Bake at 200°C/390°F for 20 minutes. Scatter the soybean sprouts over the pizza just before serving.

21 - VULCANO
VOLCANO

DOUGH:

350 G/12 OZ ALL PURPOSE FLOUR

150 G/6 OZ DURUM WHEAT FLOUR

25G BREWER'S YEARS

1 PACKET OF CUTTLEFISH INK

WATER, SALT, OLIVE OIL

TOPPING:

300 G/12 OZ CRUSHED PEELED TOMATOES (CANNED)

200 G/8 OZ CUTTLEFISH

1 DOZEN MUSSELS

4-5 ANCHOVIES

150 G/6 OZ FRESH SALMON

4 CLOVES GARLIC

MINT LEAVES

PARSLEY

DRY WHITE WINE

OLIVE OIL

Combine the two varieties of flour and place on your work table; dissolve the yeast in half a glass of water and blend it into the flour adding a pinch of salt and 5-6 tablespoons of olive oil. Dilute the cuttlefish ink in a little water and gradually add it to flour mixture. Let the dough rise for 2 ½ hours. Clean the mussels, steam them open in a skillet over a high flame, with a little olive oil, 2 cloves of garlic and a bit of parsley. Remove the shells; set the mussels aside and keep warm. Clean the cuttlefish, cut them into strips and sauté them in a skillet with 3-4 tablespoons olive oil 2 cloves garlic (remember to remove the garlic), and chopped parsley and mint leaves. After 6-7 minutes add the anchovy fillets, then add the salmon cut into strips and the mussels. Add ½ glass of dry white wine and cook for 5-6 minutes. Roll out the dough and divide it into 4 disks. Top with the crushed peeled tomatoes and the seafood. Bake at 220°C/425°F for 20 minutes.

22 - BOMBAY

DOUGH:

700 G/1 ³/₄ LB FLOUR

10 G/1 TABLESPOON DRY ACTIVATED YEAST

20G/2 TABLESPOONS CURRY POWDER

WATER, OLIVE OIL, SALT

TOPPING:

250 G/8 OZ PURÉED CRUSHED PEELED TOMATOES

1-2 RED BELL PEPPERS

1 EGGPLANT

1 ONION

200 G/8 OZ GOAT'S CHEESE

50 G/2 OZ RAISINS

OLIVE OIL

Combine the flour and dry activated yeast, then add the curry powder, olive oil and water; knead until soft and elastic. Let the dough rise for 1 ¹/₂ hours. Wash the peppers, remove the seeds and white membrane and cut them into even strips.

Wash the eggplant and slice it. Cover the slices with coarse salt (this removes the bitter taste) and let them sit for 20 minutes. Rinse the slices well and cook over the grill brushing with olive oil on both sides. Soak the raisins in lukewarm water for 10 minutes, then squeeze out the excess water. Sauté the onion in 2-3 tablespoons of olive oil. Roll out the dough, it should be thick and spread the tomatoes, salt and olive oil.

Top with the onion, eggplant slices and arrange the pepper strips to form a grid, add the chunks of cheese and the raisins. Bake at 200°C/390°F for 20 minutes. For a completely vegetarian version of this pizza, use tofu instead of the goat's cheese.

23 - AGADIR

DOUGH:

700 G/1 ¾ LB FLOUR

10 G/1 TABLESPOON DRY ACTIVATED YEAST

3 PACKETS OF SAFFRON

WATER, OLIVE OIL, SALT

SUGAR (OPTIONAL)

TOPPING:

100 G/4 OZ BEEF RUMP

100 G/4 OZ VEAL RUMP

100 G/4 OZ LEAN LAMB

100 G/4 OZ LEAN PORK

250 G/8 OZ GOAT'S CHEESE

2 CARROTS

1 ONION

3 STALKS CELERY

100 G/4 OZ PISTACHIO NUTS

GROUND RED HOT PEPPER

RED WINE

OLIVE OIL

Combine the flour and dry activated yeast, dissolve the saffron in a glass of lukewarm water and add it to the mixture along with the olive oil. Knead until soft and elastic. (If you like, you can add a pinch of sugar to the dough) Let the dough rise for 1 ½ hours. Shell and scald the pistachio nuts. Clean the vegetables and chop them into small pieces. Cut the meats into strips.

Gently sauté the chopped vegetables in 3-4 tablespoons of olive oil, toss in the meats and add a pinch of salt and a dash of ground red hot pepper. Pour a glass of red wine over the mixture and cook over a moderate flame for 10 minutes; then add the pistachio nuts.

Roll out the dough (it should not be too thick) and place it in a flat oven pan, cover it with the mixture, draining off the excess liquid, and bake at 200°C/390°F for 15 minutes. Remove from the oven and scatter chunks of the goat's milk cheese over the pizza and bake for another 5-10 minutes.

24 - PESCE SPADA E AVOCADO
SWORDFISH AND AVOCADO

DOUGH:

SEE PAGE 16, ITEM 1

TOPPING:

300 G/12 OZ CHOPPED, PEELED TOMATOES (CANNED)

300 G/12 OZ SWORDFISH STEAK

1 AVOCADO

200 G/8 OZ SOFT FRESH CHEESE

HERBS (SWEET-SCENTED VERBENA, ESTRAGON, MINT, THYME)

1 LEMON

DRY WHITE WINE

FLOUR

OLIVE OIL

Prepare the dough and let it rise for 1 hour. Finely chop the herbs and combine them with a tablespoon of floor, coat both sides of the fish with this mixture.

Heat 2-3 tablespoons of olive oil in a skillet and cook the fish for 5 minutes on each side. Drain it on a paper towel, set aside and keep warm. Cut the avocado in half, remove the pit and cut the fruit into thin slices place in a dish and pour ¹/₂ glass of white wine and a few drops of lemon juice over it.

Roll out the dough and divide it into 4 disks. Spread the tomato, season with a bit of olive oil and a dash of salt. Cut the swordfish into strips and arrange them on the pizza to form spokes as shown, garnish with chunks of cheese. Bake at 220°C/425°F for 15 minutes. Remove from the oven and place the avocado slices between the strips of fish, bake for another 5-6 minutes. Serve with olive oil on the side.

25 - POLPETTE
MEATBALL

DOUGH:

SEE PAGE 16, ITEM 1

TOPPING:

300 G/12 OZ CRUSHED PEELED TOMATOES (CANNED)

250 G/8 OZ FRESH MOZZARELLA CHEESE

250 G/8 OZ CHOPPED BEEF

1 ONION

8-10 ANCHOVIES

MUSTARD SEED

PARSLEY

RED WINE

FLOUR

VEGETABLE OIL (FOR FRYING)

OLIVE OIL

Prepare the dough and let it rise for 1 hour. While the dough is rising, wash and fillet the anchovies.

Clean the onion, chop it finely and sauté it slightly, until tender in 3-4 tablespoons of olive oil.

Add the chopped meat, salt, pepper and a sprig of chopped parsley. Add half a glass of red wine and cook slowly for 15 minutes. Set aside and let cool.

Beat the eggs, stir in the meat, if necessary, add 1 tablespoon of flour to thicken the mixture, and make little meatballs. Coat the meatballs in flour ad fry them in hot oil.

Season the tomato pulp with a little olive oil and a pinch of salt. Roll out the dough, spread the tomatoes over it, arrange the meatballs, anchovy fillets, mustard seeds and the mozzarella cut into little cubes on top. Bake at 200°C/390°F for 20 minutes.

Serve immediately.

45

26 - FOCOSA
FIERY

DOUGH:

SEE PAGE 16, ITEM 1

TOPPING:

250 G/8 OZ/DRY CHILI BEANS

100 G/4 OZ CRUSHED PEELED TOMATOES (CANNED)

200 G/8 OZ PEPPERONI SAUSAGE

250 G/8 OZ FRESH MOZZARELLA CHEESE

$^1/_2$ CARROT

$^1/_2$ ONION

1 STALK CELERY

2 CLOVES GARLIC

GROUND RED HOT PEPPER

OLIVE OIL

OLIVE OIL FLAVORED WITH RED HOT PEPPERS

Soak the beans in water for 4-5 hours. Prepare the dough and let it rise for 1 hour. Drain the beans, put them in a large pan, cover with cold water, add the carrot, onion and celery. Cook covered for 30 minutes, drain. Sauté the beans in a skillet with a little olive oil, the crushed peeled tomatoes, a pinch of salt and a dash of ground red hot pepper.

Roll out the dough and divide it into 4 disks. Top with the beans, slices of pepperoni sausage and the mozzarella cheese cut into small cubes.

Bake at 220°C/425°F for 20 minutes. Serve with the red hot pepper-flavored olive oil on the side.

27 - CAPODANNO
NEW YEAR'S EVE

DOUGH:

SEE PAGE 16, ITEM 1

TOPPING:

200 G/8 OZ CRUSH PEELED
TOMATOES (CANNED)

250 G/8 OZ FRESH MOZZARELLA
CHEESE

4 SLICES PIG'S TROTTER

200 G/8 OZ DRIED LENTILS

$^{1}/_{2}$ CARROT

1 STALK CELERY

FENNEL SEEDS (OR THYME)

OLIVE OIL

Rinse the lentils, place them in a pan, add enough cold water to cover them, add the carrot, celery, a pinch of salt and the fennel seeds (or thyme). Boil covered over a low flame for 1 $^{1}/_{2}$ hours. Drain.

Prepare the dough and let it rise for 1 hour. Put the slices of pig's trotter into a pan and cover with cold water, bring to the boil and cook for 1 hour over a moderate flame (if you use pre-cooked trotter, cooking time is reduced by half). Drain and let cool, then cut into wedges.

Roll out the dough and spread the crushed peeled tomatoes with a pinch of salt. Place the lentils on top and arrange the trotter wedges and the mozzarella cheese cut into cubes.

Add a squiggle of olive oil and sprinkle with fennel seeds (or thyme). Bake at 220°C/425°F for 20 minutes. Serve hot.

28 - SINGAPORE

DOUGH:

SEE PAGE 16, ITEM 1

TOPPING:

300 G/12 OZ CRUSHED PEELED
    TOMATOES (CANNED)

1 CHICKEN BREAST, SLICED

2 SLICES PINEAPPLE

100 G/4 OZ CASHEW NUTS

200 G/8 OZ MASCARPONE
    CHEESE

POPPY SEEDS

OLIVE OIL

Prepare the dough and let it rise for 1 hour. In the meantime, peel the pineapple slices and cut them into cubes.

Sauté the chicken breast in a skillet in a little olive oil, with salt and pepper. After 3 or 4 minutes add the pineapple chunks and cook 2 minutes longer, add the cashew nuts, stir quickly. Turn off the flame and remove the excess oil.

Roll out the dough and divide it into 4 disks. Season the tomatoes with olive oil and a pinch of salt, and spread over disks. Top with the chicken, pineapple and cashew nuts.

Bake at 220°C/425°F for 10 minutes. Remove from the oven and scatter dabs of mascarpone cheese over the tops along with poppy seeds.

Bake for another 10 minutes and serve.

29 - URBANA
URBAN

DOUGH:

SEE PAGE 16, ITEM 1

TOPPING:

250 G/8 OZ/CRUSHED PEELED
    TOMATOES (CANNED)

2 RIPE WILLIAM'S PEARS

200 G/8 OZ FRESH PECORINO
    CHEESE

RAISINS

Prepare the dough and let it rise for 1 hour. Soak the raisins in a glass of lukewarm water (25-30°C). Squeeze to remove excess water. Peel and core the pears cut them in half, and then slice thinly.

Roll out the dough, it should not be too thick, spread the tomatoes and then arrange the pears, the raisins and a pinch of salt. Bake at 200°C/390°F for 20 minutes.

Remove from the oven, and sprinkle with crumbled pecorino cheese; serve immediately.

This is an unusual pizza topping, but the combination of cheese and pears is delicious. Another, refined and excellent topping consists of fresh peas, thin slices of red skinned Stark apples, with a slightly tart flavor, and cubes of gruyere or Fontina cheese.

A totally vegetarian version consists of sliced eggplant, zucchini and tomato with a generous dousing of olive oil, and a sprinkling of fresh ginger and avocado flakes added just before serving.

30 - CANTON
CANTONESE

DOUGH:

SEE PAGE 16, ITEM 1

TOPPING:

300 G/12 OZ SOYBEAN SPROUTS

250 G/8 OZ TOFU

200 G/8 OZ FRESH PEAS
  (SHELLED)

DARK SOY SAUCE

1 LEMON

PARSLEY

SUGAR

CORIANDER SEEDS (OPTIONAL)

SUNFLOWER SEED OR OLIVE OIL

Prepare the dough and let it rise for 1 hour. Cook the peas in a little water, with a drop of oil, a teaspoon of sugar, a few parsley leaves and piece of lemon peel, with the white membrane removed, for 7-8 minutes, then drain. Heat 3-4 tablespoons of oil in a skillet and over a high flame quickly sauté the soybean sprouts, with a pinch of salt and a few drops of soy sauce, (if necessary add a tablespoon of hot water).

Roll out the dough and divide it into 4 disks and top with the crispy bean sprouts.

Scatter the peas and the tofu cut into small cubes.

If you like you can flavor the pizza with a pinch of coriander seeds.

Bake at 220°C/425°F for 20 minutes, and serve with soy sauce on the side.

31 - PORCHETTA, MOZZARELLA E POMODORO

SPICED ROAST PORK, MOZZARELLA AND TOMATO

DOUGH:

SEE PAGE 16, ITEM 1

TOPPING:

FENNEL SEEDS

250 G/8 OZ FRESH
    MOZZARELLA CHEESE

250 G/8 OZ CRUSHED, PEELED
    TOMATOES (CANNED)

400 G/14 OZ ROAST SPICED
    ROAST PORK OR LOIN OF
    PORK

300 G/12 OZ BITTER TURNIPS

1 LEMON

30 G/1 OZ BUTTER

OLIVE OIL

Prepare the dough and let it rise for 1 hour. Scrape the skin of the turnips and cook in lots of salted water with half a lemon for 20 minutes. Drain and slice into disks; sauté briefly in melted butter.

Roll out the dough thickly and spread the crushed tomatoes seasoned with a little olive oil and a pinch of salt.

Cover the pizza with thinly sliced spiced roast pork, the turnips and the mozzarella cut into cubes.

Sprinkle with fennel seeds and olive oil, bake at 220°C/425°F for 20 minutes.

32 - RENANA
RHINELAND

DOUGH:

SEE PAGE 16, ITEM 1

TOPPING:

200 G/8 OZ CRUSHED, PEELED
  TOMATOES (CANNED), PURÉED

250 G/8 OZ FRESH RED
  CABBAGE

250 G/8 OZ HEAD CABBAGE

3 LARGE FRANKFURTERS, SLICED
  LENGTHWISE

10-12 BABY CORN COBS,
  CANNED

150 G/6 OZ EMMENTHAL OR
  SIMILAR CHEESE

RED WINE VINEGAR

JUNIPER BERRIES

Prepare the dough and let it rise for 1 hour. Clean the cabbages and slice into strips, cook over a low flame for 10-12 minutes in half a ladle of hot water, a tablespoon of vinegar, 2 or 3 juniper berries and a little salt. Drain and dry.

Roll out the dough (it should be at least 1 cm or ¹/₂ inch thick) and put it into a round, oven pan; spread the tomatoes evenly.

Spread the cooked cabbage over the topping, then arrange the corn cobs alternating with the frankfurter slices to form rays.

Sprinkle with grated emmenthal and bake at 220°C/425°F for 20 minutes.

It goes without saying that the appropriate beverage for this pizza is beer.

33 - FAGIOLI, COTICHE E POMODORO
BEANS, PORK RIND AND TOMATO

DOUGH:

SEE PAGE 16, ITEM 1

TOPPING:

2 RIPE TOMATOES

250 G/8 OZ DRIED BEANS

300 G/12 OZ PORK RIND

4 CLOVES GARLIC

SAGE

OLIVE OIL

Put the beans in a large pot, and fill with water so the beans are covered, add a pinch of salt, a few sage leaves and the pork rind (rinsed under running water beforehand).

Cover and cook over a low flame for 1 hour. Drain. Cut the pork rind into strips.

In the meantime, prepare the dough and let it rise for 1 hour.

Wash the tomatoes, remove the seeds and cut them into pieces. Sauté the garlic in a skillet, with 3-4 tablespoons of olive oil, the garlic should be tender, but not browned, add the tomatoes, a few sage leaves, a pinch of salt and cook slowly until most of the liquid evaporates.

Add the beans and pork rind and cook for about 5 minutes. Drain off the excess liquid.

Roll out the dough, it should be thin and place it in a rectangular baking pan. Cover the dough with the beans and pork rind. Bake at 200°C/390°F for 20 minutes; serve immediately.

34 - PISSALADIÈRE

DOUGH:

SEE PAGE 16, ITEM 1

TOPPING:

4-5 RIPE TOMATOES

1 ONION

2 CLOVES OF GARLIC

7-8 ANCHOVIES

PITTED BLACK OLIVES

BASIL

OLIVE OIL

This is the tasty, fragrant French answer to pizza that is very similar to the pisciadela from the Liguria region of Italy.

Prepare the dough and let it rise for 1 hour. Wash and fillet the anchovies. Peel the onion and chop it finely. Clean the tomatoes and cut into little pieces.

In a skillet, with 3-4 tablespoons of olive oil sauté 1 crushed clove of garlic, remove it as soon as it starts to brown, sauté the onion until tender, add the tomatoes and cook very slowly until the liquid is absorbed.

After about 20 minutes add the anchovy fillets and let them practically dissolve.

Roll out the dough to a thickness of about 1 cm ($^1\!/_2$ inch) and divide it into 4 disks. Cover with the tomato and anchovy mixture, toss on a handful of olives and bake at 220°C/425°F for 20 minutes. Garnish with fresh basil leaves and (if you like) 1 clove of thinly sliced raw garlic.

35 - PANZEROTTI MERGELLINA

DOUGH:

SEE PAGE 16, ITEM 1

FILLING:

4-5 RIPE TOMATOES

200 G/8 OZ CRUSHED, PEELED
    TOMATOES (CANNED),
    PURÉED,

300 G/12 OZ FRESH
    MOZZARELLA CHEESE,

4-5 ANCHOVIES (OPTIONAL)

CAPERS PACKED IN VINEGAR

OREGANO, FRESH OR DRIED

OIL FOR FRYING

OLIVE OIL

Prepare the dough and let it rise for 1 hour. Clean the tomatoes. Heat 3-4 tablespoons of olive oil in a skillet, sauté the tomatoes with a pinch of salt.

Roll out the dough thinly and then cut 8-10 disks (there are over-size cookie cutters you can use).

On each disk, spread a bit of the tomato purée, the sautéed tomatoes, mozzarella cheese cut into cubes, 2-3 capers, a pinch of oregano and, if you like, an anchovy fillet. Fold in half, moisten the edges and press down firmly to seal.

Fry in oil over a moderate flame, until uniformly golden. Drain on paper towels. Spread a little tomato purée over the top of each, and add a squiggle of olive oil. Serve hot.

36 - CALZONE PARTENOPE
NEAPOLITAN CALZONE

DOUGH:

SEE PAGE 16, ITEM 1

FILLING:

4-5 RIPE TOMATOES

300 G/12 OZ FRESH
    MOZZARELLA CHEESE, SLICED
    INTO STRIPS

250 G/8 OZ RICOTTA CHEESE

150 G/6 OZ PEPPERONI
    SAUSAGE

OLIVE OIL

Prepare the dough and let it rise for 1 hour. Clean the tomatoes and cut into strips. Roll out the dough and divide it into 4 disks (diameter about 18-20 cm/8-10 inch). On each disk spread the crumbled ricotta cheese, a pinch of salt and pepperoni slices.
Fold over, moisten the edges and press firmly to seal. Dress the tops with the tomato and mozzarella slices. Bake at 220°C/425°F for 20 minutes.

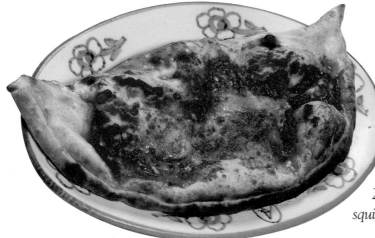

• *As to the classic calzone - that you can order in any pizzeria in Italy - nothing could be easier. On each disk of dough, place sliced ham and cubed mozzarella cheese; fold over, moisten the edges and press firmly to seal. Spread tomato puree over the top and bake at 200°C/390°F for 20 minutes. Serve hot with a squiggle of olive oil.*

37 - CALZONE FRITTO
FRIED CALZONE

DOUGH:

SEE PAGE 16, ITEM 1

FILLING:

250 G/8 OZ RICOTTA CHEESE

250 G/8 OZ SMOKED PROVOLONE OR SCAMORZA CHEESE

150 G/6 OZ PEPPERONI SAUSAGE, SLICED

OREGANO

30 G/1 OZ BUTTER

OIL FOR FRYING

Prepare the dough and let it rise for 1 hour. Remove the skin from the provolone. Put the ricotta into a bowl and blend with the butter, a bit of salt and a pinch of oregano until smooth and creamy.

Roll out the dough and divide it into 4 disks (diameter about 18-20 cm/8-10 inch). Spread the ricotta on top of each, then add chunks of provolone and the sausage slices.

Fold over, moisten the edges and press firmly to seal. Fry in oil over a moderate flame, turning carefully so they are evenly browned.

Drain on paper towels and serve hot.

38 - CALZONE TIRRENO
TYRRHENEAN CALZONE

DOUGH:

SEE PAGE 16, ITEM 1

FILLING:

500 G/1 LB MUSSELS

500 G/1 LB CLAMS

200 G/8 OZ SHELLED SHRIMP

300 G/12 OZ BABY OCTOPUS

DRY WHITE WINE

1 CLOVE GARLIC

1 GENEROUS SPRIG OF PARSLEY

OLIVE OIL

OLIVE OIL FLAVORED WITH HOT
   RED PEPPERS

Prepare the dough and let it rise for 1 hour. Clean the baby octopus and boil for 20 minutes in slightly salted water with a splash of white wine. Turn off the flame and let cool. Cut into pieces. Steam the clams and mussels open over a high flame in a pan with a clove of garlic and a little olive oil, then remove the shells.

Crush a clove of garlic and sauté it in 3-4 tablespoons of olive oil until tender, remove it as soon as it starts to brown. Add the seafood, starting with the baby octopus, then the mussels, clams and lastly the shrimps.

Pour in half a glass of white wine, add a pinch of salt and a sprig of chopped parsley. Cook slowly for 10 minutes until most of the liquid is absorbed; drain off the excess liquid.

Roll out the dough and divide it into 4 disks. Spread the seafood mixture on each disk. Fold over, moisten the edges and press firmly to seal. Bake at 220°C/425°F for 20 minutes. Serve hot with the flavored olive oil on the side.

39 - CALZONE ALLA CARNE E VERDURE
CALZONE WITH MEAT AND VEGETABLES

DOUGH:

SEE PAGE 16, ITEM 1

FILLING:

300 G/12 OZ CHOPPED BEEF

300 G/12 OZ CRUSHED, PEELED TOMATOES (CANNED)

¹/₂ CARROT

1 ONION

¹/₂ STALK CELERY

RED WINE

FLOUR, 60G

1 GLASS MILK

GRATED PARMESAN CHEESE

50 G/2 OZ BUTTER

Prepare the dough and let it rise for 1 hour. Finely chop the carrot, onion and celery, sauté in 4-5 tablespoons olive oil until tender. Add the meat and let it brown over a lively flame for 10 minutes, add a pinch of salt and half a glass of red wine.

Add the tomatoes, lower the flame and cook for about 40 minutes.

Melt the butter in a pan over a low flame, blend in the flour, gradually add 1 glass of milk, stirring constantly until the mixture thickens add a little salt and cook for another 2 minutes. Remove from stove and let cool.

Roll out the dough to a thickness of 1 cm (¹/₂ inch) and divide it into 4 disks. Spread the meat mixture over each and top with 1-2 tablespoons of the white sauce. Sprinkle with grated parmesan cheese.

Fold over, moisten the edges and press firmly to seal. Bake at 220°C/425°F for 20 minutes.

40 - FRUTTIERA
FRUITY

DOUGH:

SEE PAGE 16, ITEM 1 DO NOT
    ADD SALT

TOPPING:

250 G/8 OZ RICOTTA CHEESE

1 ORANGE

1 LEMON

2-3 GREEN PEARS

300 G/12 OZ STRAWBERRIES

1 PINEAPPLE

OTHER FRUITS IN SEASON
    (PRICKLY PEARS, GRAPES
    OR APRICOTS, CHERRIES,
    PEACHES, ETC.)

COCOA, DRY, UNSWEETENED

MILK

Did you know that pizza makes a wonderful dessert? Here's how, but remember, half a pizza should be enough for each guest.

Prepare the dough without salt and let it rise for 1 hour. Wash the fruit. Peel the pineapple and prickly pears and cut them into cubes. Slice the citrus fruits without removing the skins. Put the ricotta into a mixing bowl, add half a glass of milk, blend with a fork until you get a creamy paste. Roll out the dough and divide it into 4 disks. Spread the ricotta on each. 
Bake at 200°C/390°F for 15 minutes. Dilute 5-6 tablespoons of cocoa in half a glass of hot milk to make a thick syrup. Keep warm.
Remove the pizzas from the oven and top them with the fruit. Put them into the oven for 5 minutes; serve hot with the warm chocolate syrup.

*• When the season is right - early autumn - why not make an exquisite pizza with figs, shown here, as a meal rather than a dessert?
Prepare the four disks of dough, cover with crumbled mozzarella, add a pinch of salt and bake at 220°C/425°F for 10 minutes.
Wash 4 or 5 figs (we feel that the green skinned figs are better for this dish than the dark ones) for each pizza and cut into quarters, but do not separate the slices, so they look like little flowers. Remove the pizzas from the oven and place the cut figs on each one, along with a rolled-up slice of cured ham.
Bake for another 10 minutes and serve with flaked parmesan cheese.*

• And finally, another autumn dish. Clean 200 g/8 oz of mushrooms. Sauté them in a skillet in 2-3 tablespoons of olive oil, chopped parsley, a pinch of salt and a dash of pepper. Top the pizza disks with ricotta or mozzarella cheese, then add the mushrooms, walnut halves, and sprigs of rosemary.
Bake at 200°C/390°F for 20 minutes.
Garnish with fresh parsley as shown and serve.

SAUCES

"GENOVESE"
GENOESE

1 KG/2 LB BEEF

SLICED BACON

50 G/2 OZ BUTTER

2 TEASPOONS TOMATO
  CONCENTRATE

1 DL/ ½ CUP OLIVE OIL

2 GLASSES RED WINE

1,5 KG/ 3 LB ONIONS

1 STALK CELERY

1 CARROT

BEEF BROTH OR WATER

Peel the onions and slice. Wrap the bacon slices around the meat and tie with string. Put the onions into a pan with the carrots, chopped celery and the meat. Add the butter and olive oil and cook over a moderate flame for 2 hours. Raise the flame, add the tomato concentrate and stir with a wooden spoon. Add the wine, at little at a time, letting it evaporate after each addition. Add the broth or lukewarm water and cook, uncovered over a very low flame. This will make the meat absorb all the flavors. Remove the meat and put it on a serving platter. Add broth or water to the sauce in the pan and continue cooking slowly until it is shiny or the onions are liquefied.

GLASSA

500 G/1 LB BEEF

100 G/4 OZ BACON

100 G/4 OZ BUTTER

1 TEASPOON TOMATO
CONCENTRATE

75 G/ $^1/_3$ CUP OLIVE OIL

1 BOUQUET (1 CARROT, 1 STALK
CELERY, 1 ONION, 1 SPRIG
OF PARSLEY)

WHITE WINE, 1 GLASS

BEEF BROTH OR WATER

Trim the fat off the meat, wrap it in the bacon slices and tie with string. Put the meat into a large pan along with the olive oil, butter and bouquet. Cover and cook over a very low flame for about 1 hour, stirring every now and then. When the vegetables start to brown add the white wine and tomato concentrate. Stir and continue cooking, add broth or water, letting the liquid evaporate almost entirely between additions. As soon as the meat is tender, test it with a fork, raise the flame so that it will brown evenly. Remove the meat; it is excellent with a variety of side dishes. Put the sauce through a sieve before using.

RAGÙ CLASSICO NAPOLETANO
CLASSIC NEAPOLITAN MEAT SAUCE

1 KG/2 LB MEAT (BEEF)

SLICED BACON

50 G/2 OZ LARD

600 G/21 OZ TOMATO

CONCENTRATE

4 TABLESPOONS OLIVE OIL

2 GLASSES RED WINE

350 G/13 OZ ONIONS

Wrap the bacon around the meat and tie with string. Wash and slice the onions very thinly. Put the onions and meat into a pot (earthenware is best) with the olive oil and lard.

Cook the meat slowly, turning it with a wooden spoon so that it browns evenly and does not stick to the pot. Stir the onions and add a little red wine every now and then to keep them from burning.

After about 1 hour, the meat should be evenly browned and the onions dissolved.

Remove the meat and set it aside. The next phase is rather time consuming and is the key to a perfect Neapolitan meat sauce or "ragu".

Gradually add the tomato concentrate to the sauce left in the pot, stirring constantly. Raise the flame and as soon as you notice that the concentrate starts to stick to the pot, add the red wine a little at a time, stirring all the while until the concentrate has turned to a dark color.

Now, put the meat back into the pot, cover with lukewarm water and salt to taste. Lower the flame, cover the pot partly, so that air can escape and let the sauce simmer. Remember to keep an eye on it. Test the meat with a fork, when it is tender remove it from the pot.

Let the sauce simmer longer until it is dark red. Use a slotted spoon to skim off the excess fat that tends to float to the top of the sauce.

This is the authentic Neapolitan ragu and it takes about 6 hours to prepare.

Very few people take the time to make it these days, but if you do, you will see that it is worth every minute that goes into it.

RAGÙ FINTO
MEAT SAUCE

500 G/1 LB LOIN OF PORK,
OR VARIOUS MEATS,

200 G/8 OZ TOMATO
CONCENTRATE

100 G/4 OZ OLIVE OIL OR
LARD

RED WINE, 1 GLASS

Put the meat into a pan with the olive oil or lard and brown it gradually, until it forms a crust. Without turning off the flame, remove the meat and put it aside. Add the tomato concentrate to the contents of the pan, and add a little red wine now and then to keep it from burning. The tomato concentrate will quickly become creamy and brownish. Add hot water and salt, mix well and put the meat back into the pan. Let it simmer for about 2 hours. The sauce should be reasonably thick. If you want to use for oven-baked pasta dishes, keep it thinner and more fluid because baking tends to dry out the ingredients.

SALSA CON FILETTI DI POMODORO
TOMATO STRIPS

700 G/1 ³/₄ LB TOMATOES

GARLIC, ONION, CARROT,
CELERY

OLIVE OIL

SALT

Wash the tomatoes, the San Marzano or plum tomatoes are the best, dip them into boiling water for a few minutes. Remove, drain, peel and remove the seeds taking care not to cut them too deeply. Drain and dry them thoroughly. In a deep skillet, sauté the vegetables until just barely golden, add the tomatoes and stir with a whisk to get the right consistency. Cook for about 20 minutes.

SALSA DI CONCENTRATO
TOMATO CONCENTRATE SAUCE

250 G/8 OZ TOMATO
CONCENTRATE

50 G/2 OZ OLIVE OIL

RED WINE

WATER

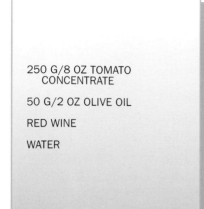

Heat the olive oil in a pan and add the tomato concentrate; stir with a wooden spoon and gradually add the red wine (or just hot water if you prefer), to keep it from sticking.

Let it simmer for a few minutes, salt to taste and dilute with hot water.

Cover the pan and let it simmer for about 2 hours. The sauce tends to burn, add hot water as needed and stir occasionally.

The sauce will be ready when the oil floats to the top and the overall consistency is creamy.

SALSA CON I POMODORINI DI SORRENTO
SORRENTO TOMATO SAUCE

700 G/1 ¾ LB TOMATOES

OLIVE OIL

2 CLOVES GARLIC

PARSLEY OR BASIL

OREGANO

SUGAR

Wash the tomatoes and cut them in half. Chop the garlic and heat it in a skillet with the olive oil, add the tomatoes, salt to taste and add a pinch of sugar. Cook over a lively flame for 10 minutes, stirring constantly.

To give the sauce a more distinctive flavor, add a little chopped parsley or basil, as you prefer, and a dash of oregano.

Do not be concerned if, during cooking the tomato peels tend to detach and form tiny little rolls, you will not notice them when you use the sauce.

SALSA DI POMODORO FRESCO
FRESH TOMATO SAUCE

500 G/1 LB TOMATOES,

OLIVE OIL

BASIL

SALT

SUGAR

Wash the tomatoes (San Marzano or plum tomatoes are the best), cut them lengthwise and put them in a pan with the basil, a dash of salt and pinch of sugar, cover and simmer. As soon as the tomatoes are soft lower the flame, uncover and cook slowly until the liquid evaporates. Use the finest sieve and put the tomatoes through the food mill.

The result will be "tomato purée", a light and tasty sauce ideal for dressing pasta and for preparing many other dishes.

SALSA PIZZAIOLA
PIZZAIOLA SAUCE

600 G/ FLANK STEAK, SLICED

500 G/1 LB PEELED
   TOMATOES,

75 G/3 OZ OLIVE OIL

1 CLOVE GARLIC, CHOPPED

PARSLEY

OREGANO

Trim the fat off the meat. In a large saucepan combine the peeled tomatoes (canned or fresh, though the latter are preferable), the garlic, olive oil and salt to taste, add the meat. Cook covered, over a moderate flame for about 1 hour. The sauce will be ready when it is thick and dark.

A suggestion: before serving, check for salt, and give it a touch of originality with a sprinkling of oregano and chopped parsley.

If you want to use the sauce to dress pasta (it is perfect for spaghetti and linguine), use 700 g/1 ³/₄ lb. of tomatoes.

DOUGHS

PASTA FROLLA
SHORT PASTRY

INGREDIENTS FOR 6

500 G/1 LB FLOUR

4 EGG YOLKS

250 G/8 OZ LARD

150 G/6 OZ SUGAR

1 ORANGE, SQUEEZED

Combine the lard, sugar, egg yolks and a pinch of salt with the flour on the work table. Blend with a fork, and moisten the dough with the orange juice. To obtain the right consistency, knead it with your hands. Shape the dough into a ball, cover it with a clean, damp cloth and let it rest for at least 30 minutes.

Short pastry dough tends to behave badly when you roll it out. To prevent it from breaking into *a thousand pieces, roll it out on a sheet of oven paper so that you can turn it right into your baking* *pan without having to handle it too much.*

PASTA MEZZA FROLLA
LIGHT SHORT PASTRY

INGREDIENTS FOR 6

500 G/1 LB FLOUR

2 EGG YOLKS

100 G/4 OZ BUTTER

SUGAR

WATER

This is a fine and lighter alternative to short pastry for those who prefer less striking flavor contrasts.

Prepare the dough exactly the same way as the short pastry, but use cold water instead of orange juice to moisten it.

PASTA BRISÉE
PLAIN PASTRY

INGREDIENTS FOR 6

500 G/1 LB FLOUR

250 G/8 OZ BUTTER

2 DL/ 1 CUP ICE WATER

Pour half of the ice water into the middle of the flour on the work table. Add the butter, which because of the icy water will not melt immediately. Keep kneading the dough, adding a little ice water now and then. When the dough is firm sprinkle it with flour, wrap it in a clean dry cloth and let it rest in a moderately cool place for about 2 hours. Roll out the dough with a floured rolling pin.

PASTA DI PANE
BREAD DOUGH

INGREDIENTS FOR 6

500 G/1 LB FLOUR

BREWER'S YEAST

1/2 GLASS OLIVE OIL

LUKEWARM WATER

Dissolve the yeast in a little lukewarm water, use a fork to help. Pour the dissolved yeast, olive oil and a pinch of salt into the middle of the flour mounded on your work table. Knead it vigorously to obtain a soft, elastic dough.

Let it rise for about 30 minutes or even 45 minutes until it is soft and elastic. Flour the work table and roll out the dough.

SOUPS AND BROTHS

MINESTRA CON CICORIA E "SCAROLELLE"
CHICORY AND ESCAROLE SOUP

600 G/24 OZ BEEF

1.250 KG/1³/₄ LB ESCAROLE AND CHICORY

100 G/4 OZ PARMESAN AND PECORINO CHEESE, GRATED, PLUS TWO PARMESAN CHEESE CRUSTS

1 CLOVE GARLIC

1 BOUQUET (1 CARROT, 1 STALK CELERY, 1 ONION, PARSLEY)

This recipe is a simple variation of chicory soup, but the flavor is more intense because it is made with meat broth, and fresh, young escarole, that is a part of Neapolitan culinary tradition.

First prepare the broth. Boil the beef with the bouquet, garlic, olive oil and a pinch of salt. Then pass it through a sieve and skim off the fat.
Carefully clean and wash the chicory and escarole, scald briefly in salted water, and drain carefully. Cook the chicory and escarole in the broth, and add part of the meat (cut into little pieces) that you used to make the broth. Serve hot with a generous dusting of parmesan and pecorino.

MINESTRA DI FAGIOLINI AL POMODORO
GREEN BEAN AND TOMATO SOUP

1 KG/2 LB GREEN BEANS

0.75 L/3 PINTS TOMATO PURÉE

50 G/2 OZ OLIVE OIL

BASIL

SUGAR

Prepare a fresh tomato sauce using the recipe on page 69, make sure that the sauce is quite fluid.
In the meantime, clean the green beans, cut off the ends and remove the "string", and wash them.
Cook the beans in salted water.

When they are done, add them to the tomato sauce and boil covered for about 1 hour.
Garnish with fresh basil leaves before serving.

MINESTRA DI LENTICCHIE
LENTIL SOUP

350 G/13 OZ LENTILS

2 PEELED TOMATOES

100 G/4 OZ OLIVE OIL

1 CLOVE GARLIC, CUT UP

PARSLEY

Clean and wash the lentils; boil them in a partly covered pot over a moderate flame.

When the lentils are done, add the tomatoes, garlic and olive oil, salt to taste.

Boil for about 20 minutes, then garnish with a bit of chopped parsley.

If the soup seems too thick, you can dilute it by adding a little hot water.

MINESTRA "MARITATA"
WINTER SOUP

INGREDIENTS FOR 10

1 KG/2 LB BEEF

1 KG/2 LB LOIN OF PORK

1 PIG TAIL

1 HAMBONE

200 G/8 OZ LEAN HAM

200 G/8 OZ HAM RIND

300 G/12 OZ SAUSAGE

300 G/12 OZ SPICY
    NEAPOLITAN SAUSAGE

1 SMALL CHICKEN

300 G/12 OZ BORAGE

500 G/1 LB CHICORY LEAVES

1 KG/2 LB ESCAROLE

2 MEDIUM SAVOY CABBAGES

150 G/6 OZ PARMESAN CHEESE

100 G/4 OZ AGED
    CACIOCAVALLO CHEESE

Boil the beef, chicken and pork in separate pots. Remember to put the pork into cold water, starting with the saltiest parts, such as the hambone. When the water is hot, drain and fill the pot with cold water; repeat 3 times. Lastly add the pig tail and loin. In another pot boil all the vegetables together; when they are cooked, drain and squeeze out the excess water. You will now have 4 different types of broth: skim off the surface fat. Combine them in a large pot, add the vegetables and simmer for a few hours, stirring now and then so that they absorb all the flavors. Toss in the boiled pork just before serving. Each guest can grate cheese onto the soup according to taste.

"Maritata" soup is the most classic of Neapolitan winter soups. It is a "marriage" of meats and vegetables. The meats can be used in various ways.

MINESTRA DI RISO CON VERZE
RICE AND CABBAGE SOUP

350 G/13 OZ RICE

400 G/14 OZ SAVOY CABBAGE

100 G/4 OZ BACON

50 G/2 OZ PARMESAN CHEESE, GRATED, PLUS 2 CRUSTS

50 G/2 OZ PECORINO CHEESE, GRATED

1.5 L/1.5 QT MEAT BROTH

2 TABLESPOONS OLIVE OIL

1 ONION

WHITE WINE

Wash and cut the cabbage into medium size chunks.

Scrape the cheese crusts clean.

Chop the onion and bacon coarsely and then sauté in a large pot with a little olive oil, add white wine gradually. When the mixture is golden, add half the broth and bring to the boil, lower the flame. Add the cabbage and the two cheese crusts.

Cook covered for about 30 minutes. Add the rice and cook, stirring constantly, keep on adding broth so that the soup mixture does not dry.

The soup will be ready when the rice has absorbed all the liquid.

Serve hot with a sprinkling of parmesan and pecorino cheese.

MINESTRA DI ZUCCHINE AL POMODORO
ZUCCHINI AND TOMATO SOUP

1 KG/2 LB ZUCCHINI

TOMATO SAUCE, SEE PAGE 69

PARMESAN CHEESE

BASIL

Prepare 1.5 liters/ 1.5 quarts of tomato sauce according to the recipe on page 69.
Clean the zucchini, cut them into chunks, boil for a few minutes, remove and drain.
Add the zucchini to the tomato sauce. Cover and cook for 15 minutes.
When the zucchini have absorbed the sauce, flavor with a generous sprinkling of grated parmesan cheese and basil, stir well and serve hot.

SAUTÉ DI VONGOLE
CLAM SAUTÉ

Soak the clams in salted water for at least 4 hours to remove all the sand. Drain well. Sauté the garlic in a skillet and add the clams, sprinkle with a little chopped parsley, cover and cook for a few minutes.

1.5 KG /3 LB CLAMS

2 TOMATOES

1 DL/ ½ CUP OLIVE OIL

2 CLOVES GARLIC

PARSLEY

WHITE WINE, 1 GLASS

Check the clams and remove them as they open, and set them aside.
When all the clams are open, put them back into the skillet, add the fresh tomatoes cut into chunks, and the white wine, cook over a moderate flame. As soon as the clams are hot, remove from the stove, garnish with chopped parsley and serve.

ZUPPA DI COZZE ROSSA
RED MUSSEL SOUP

2 KG/4 LB MUSSELS

750 G/ ¾ LB PEELED TOMATOES

1 DL/ ½ CUP OLIVE OIL

2 CLOVES GARLIC

GROUND RED HOT PEPPER

Clean the mussels thoroughly, scrape off the encrustations and rinse repeatedly until the water runs clean.

Heat the garlic and olive oil in a large pan. When the garlic is lightly browned, add the mussels and tomatoes. Cover and cook over a high flame for 10 minutes. Remove the mussels as they open and set them aside. When you have taken out all the mussels let the sauce cook and thicken for a few minutes, then put back the mussels and simmer for a few minutes. Serve hot and season with a pinch of ground red hot pepper.

Croutons are an excellent complement to this soup.

ZUPPA DI FAGIOLI
BEAN SOUP

400 G/14 OZ BEANS

5-6 PEELED TOMATOES

1 DL/ ½ CUP OLIVE OIL

1 CLOVE GARLIC, CRUSHED

PARSLEY

1 STALK CELERY

1 RED HOT PEPPER

In a skillet slightly brown the garlic and red hot pepper in the olive oil, remove as soon they are browned.

Add the tomatoes and parsley, salt and cook for 5 minutes. In the meantime clean the celery and cook it with the beans. Cook the beans in a small amount of water over a moderate flame (a covered earthenware pot is best).

Make sure that the water does not evaporate entirely, add more as needed. When the beans are nearly done, add the tomato sauce and blend. Cook for a few more minutes over a moderate flame.

ZUPPA FORTE O ZUPPA DI SOFFRITTO
HEARTY SOUP

INGREDIENTS FOR 6

1 KG/2 LB PORK LIVER AND LIGHTS

1 L/1 QT TOMATO PUREE

140 G/5 OZ TOMATO CONCENTRATE

50 G/2 OZ LARD

3 RED HOT PEPPERS

BAY LEAVES

Combine tomato concentrate and the red hot peppers, to make a hot, spicy base known as "salsa forte".

Wash the pork liver and lights in cold water and cut into small pieces.

Heat the lard in a skillet and add the pork. When it is thoroughly browned add 2 or 3 bay leaves and the tomato-hot pepper mixture. Stir until thick, then add the tomato puree, salt to taste, and cook, covered over a low flame for 30 minutes. Serve over toasted bread.

This rich soup is a fine dish in winter. If you want to use it to dress pasta, cook it until it thickens and is not runny.

ZUPPA DI PESCE
FISH SOUP

INGREDIENTS FOR 10

1 KG/2.2 LB "TUB FISH"

1.5 KG/3 LB OCTOPUS, SQUID AND CUTTLEFISH

1 KG/2 LB SCORPION FISH

1 KG/2 LB MUSSELS

500 G/1 LB CLAMS

1 KG/2 LB PEELED TOMATOES

TOASTED BREAD

2 DL/1 CUP OLIVE OIL

2 CLOVES GARLIC

PARSLEY

Simmer the peeled tomatoes and garlic in a large saucepan to make a tasty sauce. In the meantime, clean the fish, seafood and shellfish. Place the washed clams and mussels in a pot without water, cover and cook over a very low flame until they open and release all their liquid. Collect the liquid and strain it through cheesecloth.

Add the squid, octopus and cuttlefish to the tomato sauce, cook for about twenty minutes and then add the fish, gradually add the liquid from the clams and mussels. When just about done, add the clams, mussels and a generous amount of chopped parsley. Serve hot with crispy toasted bread.

Scorpion and "tub fish" are just two varieties that can be used in this soup. It all depends on your personal preferences. It is important to use fish that are about the same size; if you use large fish, it is better to cut them into pieces.

ZUPPA DI "SPULLECARIELLI"
FRESH BEAN SOUP

INGREDIENTS FOR 6

1.5 KG/3 LB FRESH BEANS, SHELLED

250 G/8 OZ FRESH TOMATOES

100 G/4 OZ OLIVE OIL

2 CLOVES GARLIC

BASIL

CELERY

RED HOT PEPPER

OREGANO

Shell the beans. In Naples unshelled beans are called "spullecarielli", shelled they become "fagioli" the word everyone knows!

Cook the beans with the celery for about 2 hours, and follow the instructions for bean soup on page 84.

Remember to use basil instead of parsley, and then just before serving add 1 more basil leaf and a pinch of oregano.

ZUPPA DI STOCCAFISSO
DRIED CODFISH SOUP

1.250 KG/2.5 LB DRIED
   CODFISH

TOMATO SAUCE, SEE PAGE 69

50 G/2 OZ OLIVE OIL

PARSLEY

BASIL

Prepare the tomato sauce according the recipe on page 69. Dip the codfish into boiling water for a couple of minutes; drain and clean it, removing the skin and backbone, and cut it into medium size chunks.

Add the codfish to the tomato sauce and cook until tender and the sauce has thickened.

Salt to taste and sprinkle with a little chopped parsley just before serving.

To make this codfish soup a delicious main course dilute the tomato sauce with a little water and add 1.250 kg or 2 ¹/₂ lb of peeled, cubed potatoes. Add the codfish when the potatoes are nearly done.

PASTA DISHES

LINGUINE AL SUGO DI "CUOCCIO"
LINGUINE IN "TUB FISH" SAUCE

400 G/14 OZ LINGUINE

1 KG/2 LBS "TUB FISH"

500 G/1 LB PEELED
  TOMATOES

1 DL/ ½ CUP OLIVE OIL

2 CLOVES GARLIC

PARSLEY, CHOPPED

BASIL

1 RED HOT PEPPER, CRUSHED

Cut the tomatoes in half lengthwise, place in a pot with the parsley, garlic, olive oil, a little of the crushed red hot pepper and the "tub fish". Cover firmly with a sheet of aluminum foil and cook over a very low flame.

When the fish is tender, add a pinch of salt. Take out the fish and remove the backbone and cut it into small pieces. Put the cut fish into a double boiler with a little of the cooking sauce and keep warm.

Let the rest of the sauce simmer until it thickens.

Cook the linguine in salted water until they are *al dente*, drain and add to the sauce.

Mix well, add a bit of basil and place on a serving dish, top with more sauce and the fish.

"Tub fish" is just one variety of fish you can use, grouper and scorpion fish are also excellent.

LINGUINE AI POLPI VERACI
LINGUINE WITH OCTOPUS

400 G/14 OZ LINGUINE

1 KG/2 LB OCTOPUS

1 KG/2 LB PEELED TOMATOES

1 DL/ ½ CUP OLIVE OIL

2 CLOVES GARLIC

PARSLEY, CHOPPED

GROUND RED HOT PEPPER

Clean and wash the octopus, place them in a saucepan with the tomatoes, garlic, olive oil and a dash of ground red hot pepper. Cook covered for 1 hour.

Cook the linguine in boiling, salted water. Drain.

When the octopus are tender, remove the pan, add a dash of salt to the sauce and use it to dress the linguine.

For an added touch of flavor, garnish with chopped parsley just before serving.

If the octopus are very small, you can use them with the sauce to dress the pasta, otherwise, they make a fine second course.

LINGUINE MEZZODÌ
LINGUINE SOUTHERN STYLE

400 G/14 OZ LINGUINE

4-5 RIPE TOMATOES

1 EGGPLANT

1 PEPPER

OLIVE OIL

1 CLOVE GARLIC, CRUSHED

BASIL

SAGE AND ROSEMARY
    (OPTIONAL)

2 ANCHOVIES

OLIVES, PITTED AND CHOPPED

CAPERS

Wash the tomatoes, cut them open, remove the seeds and then cut them into pieces.

Wash and cube the eggplant.

Wash the pepper, remove the seeds and white membrane and cut into strips.

Wash, filet and cut up the anchovies.

Sauté the garlic in 5-6 tablespoons olive oil, until golden, remove it and add the tomatoes and eggplant.

When the eggplant is tender, add the pepper, olives, a tablespoon of drained capers and the and the anchovies.

Simmer for a few minutes and salt to taste.

Cook the linguine *al dente*, drain and place in a serving bowl, pour the sauce over the pasta and add a sprinkling of fresh basil.

If you like the aroma, you can garnish it with a few sprigs of rosemary and sage.

SPAGHETTI CAPO MISENO

400 G/14 OZ SPAGHETTI

TOMATO SAUCE

250 G/8 OZ FRESH MOZZARELLA
CHEESE, SLICED

STUFFED OLIVES, HALVED

THYME

60 G/2 OZ BUTTER, MELTED

FOR THE MEATBALLS:

400 G/14 OZ /1 ³/₄ CUPS
CHOPPED BEEF

1 WHOLE EGG AND 1 YOLK

2 CLOVES GARLIC, CHOPPED

1 SPRIG PARSLEY, CHOPPED

BREAD CRUMBS

OIL FOR FRYING

Combine the meat, egg, yolk, garlic and parsley in a bowl and blend well. Shape into little balls and coat with bread crumbs.

Fry the meatballs in hot oil over a moderate flame. Drain on paper towels.

Cook the spaghetti in boiling salted water for 6-7 minutes. Drain. Put the spaghetti in an oven dish and top with the tomato sauce, meatballs, olives and mozzarella.

Pour the melted butter over the spaghetti and bake at 200°C/390°F for 8-10 minutes, or until the mozzarella melts.

SPAGHETTI ALLA SPICCIA
QUICK SPAGHETTI

400 G/14 OZ SPAGHETTI

2 ANCHOVIES

2 RIPE TOMATOES

1 SPRIG BASIL, CHOPPED

1 CLOVE GARLIC, CHOPPED

OREGANO

1 SPRIG PARSLEY, CHOPPED

DRY WHITE WINE

OLIVE OIL

Wash the tomatoes, cut them in half, remove the seeds and cut into chunks. Wash the anchovies under running water, open them and cut them up.

Sauté the chopped basil, parsley and garlic in 4-5 tablespoons of olive oil, add half a glass of white wine and let it evaporate. Add the tomatoes, anchovies and a dash of oregano, salt and pepper to taste and cook over a high flame for about 5 minutes.

Before the sauce is done, cook the spaghetti in boiling, salted water until they are *al dente*, drain. Put the spaghetti into a serving bowl, top with the sauce and mix well. If you like, you can serve it with a sprinkling of parmesan cheese, but for this dish the cheese is truly optional.

VERMICELLI BELLA NAPOLI

350 G/13 OZ VERMICELLI

4-5 RIPE TOMATOES, CUBED

1 CLOVE GARLIC, CRUSHED

MARJORAM

GRATED PARMESAN CHEESE

OLIVE OIL

Sauté the garlic in a skillet with 5-6 tablespoons olive oil. Remove the garlic as soon as it starts to brown and add the tomatoes. Salt and pepper to taste and simmer for about 20 minutes.

Cook the pasta in boiling salted water until it is *al dente*, drain. Put it in a serving bowl and top with the sauce. Add a generous sprinkling of grated cheese and garnish with fresh marjoram leaves.

VERMICELLI IN CARTOCCIO
VERMICELLI BAKED IN PAPER

INGREDIENTS FOR 4-6

400 G/14 OZ VERMICELLI

500 G/1 LB MUSSELS

500 G/1 LB. BABY OCTOPUS

500 G/1 LB CLAMS

1 KG/2 LB PEELED TOMATOES

OLIVE OIL

GARLIC

BASIL

GROUND RED HOT PEPPER

Put the clams and mussels into a pan, cover and cook over a very low flame until the shells have opened.

Remove the shells. Collect the liquid and pass it through cheese cloth and set aside.

In a saucepan combine the tomatoes, basil, garlic, olive oil and ground red hot pepper. Dilute with the liquid from the clams and mussels and add the baby octopus and cook until tender. Add the clams and mussels, and remove from the stove.

In the meantime, cook the vermicelli in boiling salted water until they are *al dente*, drain.

Dress the pasta with the sauce and place into stiff, oven paper, fold over and close.

Bake in warm oven for 15 minutes and serve hot, open the wrapper at the table.

PERCIATELLI CAPODIMONTE

400 G/14 OZ PERCIATELLI

100 G/4 OZ SALAMI, THINLY SLICED

4-5 RIPE TOMATOES

1 ONION, CHOPPED

DRY WHITE WINE

150 G/6 OZ MILD PROVOLONE CHEESE, 1 SLICE CUT INTO STRIPS

GRATED PARMESAN CHEESE

SAGE

OLIVE OIL

Wash the tomatoes, remove the seeds, cut into chunks. Sauté the onion and a sprig of sage in 4-5 tablespoons olive oil. Add the salami, and after a few minutes add 1 glass white wine. When the wine has evaporated lower the flame, add the tomatoes and a pinch of salt, cook for about 15 minutes.

Cook the perciatelli in boiling salted water until they are *al dente*, drain. Place in a serving bowl and top with the tomato sauce, be sure to remove the sage leaves. Garnish with grated parmesan cheese and scatter the provolone strips over it all.

Perciatelli is a hollow pasta, each one is about 25 cm long and about 5 mm in diameter; they resemble bucatini which are not more 3 mm in diameter.

SPAGHETTI ALLA "CHIUMMENZANA"

400 G/14 OZ SPAGHETTI

TOMATO SAUCE, PAGE 68

OREGANO

Prepare the tomato sauce following the recipe on page 68. In the meantime, cook the spaghetti in boiling salted water until they are *al dente*, drain.

Put the spaghetti into the pan with the sauce, mix quickly with a fork, garnish with fresh basil and a pinch of oregano.

Serve immediately.

"Chiummenzana" is the Neapolitan word for those wonderful tiny little tomatoes that are picked before they are fully ripened and hung in small bunches.

VERMICELLI A' PUVURIELLO

350 G/13 OZ VERMICELLI

4 EGGS

30 G/1 OZ LARD

100 G GRATED PARMESAN CHEESE

1 DL/ 1/2 CUP OLIVE OIL

2 CLOVES GARLIC, CRUSHED

Gently sauté the garlic in a skillet with the olive oil and lard.

In a bowl, beat the eggs and add a pinch of salt and dash of pepper.

Cook the vermicelli in boiling, salted water until they are *al dente*, drain.

Pour the hot oil, eggs and cheese onto the pasta, mix well and serve piping hot.

If you prefer, you can substitute caciocavallo cheese for the parmesan.

FUSILLI ALLA VESUVIANA

INGREDIENTS FOR 6

400 G/14 OZ FUSILLI

1 KG/2 LB PEELED TOMATOES

OLIVE OIL

2 CLOVES GARLIC

PARSLEY, CHOPPED

1 RED HOT PEPPER, CHOPPED

200 G/8 OZ PITTED GREEN OLIVES

50 G/2 OZ CAPERS

Sauté the garlic in a little olive oil, add the peeled tomatoes and cook for 15 minutes. Add the capers, olives and the red hot pepper; cook for another 15 minutes.

In the meantime, cook the fusilli in boiling, salted water until they are *al dente*, drain and dress with the sauce.

Sprinkle with the chopped parsley and serve hot.

GNOCCHI O STRANGOLAPRETI AL POMODORO
POTATO DUMPLINGS WITH TOMATO SAUCE

INGREDIENTS FOR 8

TOMATO SAUCE, PAGE 69

1 KG/2 LB POTATOES

600 G/20 OZ FLOUR

1 EGG

30 G/1 OZ BUTTER

GRATED PARMESAN CHEESE

OLIVE OIL

Prepare the gnocchi, which are little potato dumplings according to the recipe on page 104.

Prepare the tomato sauce according to the recipe on page 69.

To cook the gnocchi, slide from a plate them into boiling, salted water, a few at a time, and remove them with a slotted spoon as they float to the top.

When they are all drained, put them into a serving bowl with the butter, stir gently and top with the tomato sauce. Serve grated parmesan cheese on the side.

According to Neapolitan tradition, these gnocchi can also be served with the classic meat sauce.

GNOCCHI ALLA SORRENTINA
POTATO DUMPLINGS ALLA SORRENTINA

1.2 KG/ 2 ½ LB POTATOES

300 G/12 OZ FRESH
 MOZZARELLA CHEESE,
 CUBED

800G/2 LB FLOUR

700 G/1 ¾ LB TOMATO
 PUREE, SEE PAGE 69

1 EGG

GRATED PARMESAN CHEESE

Prepare the tomato sauce according to the recipe on page 69.
Boil the potatoes in the jackets. When they are tender, peel and put through a fine ricer.
Combine the potatoes, flour, egg and a pinch of salt until well blended, the mixture should be soft and homogeneous.
Take a little of the mixture, and on a floured surface roll into a little rod. Repeat until you have used all the mixture. Now, cut the rods into pieces about 1.5-2 cm (¾ inch) long. Press them light with the back of a fork, or with your finger. Lay them out neatly on a floured cloth.
Bring a full pot of water to the boil slide the gnocchi into the water, a few at a time, and remove them with a slotted spoon as they float to the top.
When they are all drained, place them in an oven dish, top with the tomato sauce, the mozzarella and grated parmesan. Bake in a hot oven for 5 minutes.

MACCHERONI "LARDIATI"
MACARONI DRESSED WITH LARD

400 G/14 OZ MACARONI

100 G/4 OZ GRATED PECORINO
 CHEESE

250 G/8 OZ LARD, CUT INTO
 SMALL PIECES

Cook the macaroni in boiling salted water. In a saucepan, cook the lard over a very low flame until it melts, and only the golden, crispy scraps called "ciccioli" remain.
Drain the macaroni and pour it into the pan with the lard, add half the grated cheese and a dash of pepper.
Serve hot and top with the rest of the cheese.

MACCHERONI CON RICOTTA E SALSICCE IN BIANCO

MACARONI WITH RICOTTA CHEESE AND SAUSAGE

400 G/14 OZ MACARONI

300 G/12 OZ SAUSAGE

300 G/12 OZ RICOTTA CHEESE

GRATED PARMESAN CHEESE

Cook the macaroni in boiling salted water; use a ladle to take off a little of the water. Drain the macaroni.

Add this water to the ricotta and mix with a fork until it is creamy.

Prick the sausages with a fork and brown lightly in a skillet. Skin the sausages and cut them into medium-thick slices.

Place the sausage slices in a serving bowl, add the macaroni and the ricotta. Add the hot cooking liquid from the sausage and mix gently.

Serve with grated parmesan cheese on the side.

MEZZANELLI ALLA SCARPARIELLO

INGREDIENTS FOR 6

400 G/14 OZ MEZZANELLI

750 G/ 1 3/4 LB PEELED
 TOMATOES, SLICED

250 G/8 OZ FRESH
 MOZZARELLA CHEESE,
 CUBED

50 G/2 OZ GRATED PARMESAN
 CHEESE

OLIVE OIL

2 CLOVES GARLIC

1 SPRIG FRESH BASIL,
 CHOPPED

In skillet, sauté the garlic in olive oil until golden, add the tomatoes and cook for 10 minutes. Add the basil and cook 10 minutes more.

Cook the mezzanelli in boiling salted water until they are *al dente*, drain. Put the pasta into a serving bowl, add the mozzarella and the tomato sauce. Stir until all the ingredients are well blended; serve with grated parmesan cheese.

MEZZANI CAPODIMONTE

400 G/14 OZ MEZZANI

4 RIPE TOMATOES

200 G/8 OZ PITTED GREEN AND
    BLACK OLIVES

FRESH OREGANO

BREAD CRUMBS

1 RED HOT PEPPER, CHOPPED

OLIVE OIL

Wash the tomatoes and scald in boiling water, peel, remove the seeds and cut them into cubes.

Grease an oven dish with olive oil, add the tomatoes, olives and red hot pepper.

Cook the mezzani in boiling salted water until they are a little less than *al dente*, drain and place in the oven dish.

Add a squiggle of olive oil, a pinch of oregano and mix until all the ingredients are well blended.

Scatter with bread crumbs and bake at 200°C/390°F for 10 minutes.

Serve hot. This dish is as graceful and delicate as the porcelain from which it gets its name. No cheese is needed, in fact, it is not even recommended, but, if you prefer...

MEZZANI ALLA SALSA "GENOVESE"
MEZZANI IN GENOESE SAUCE

400 G/14 OZ MEZZANI,

GENOESE SAUCE, SEE PAGE 64

Prepare the Genoese sauce according to the recipe on page 64 (this sauce may be called Genoese, but it is unheard of in Genoa's region of Liguria!).

Break the mezzani and cook in boiling salted water until they are *al dente*, drain. Put the pasta in a serving bowl and top with the sauce, serve hot.

PENNETTE "SCIUÉ SCIUÉ"

400 G/14 OZ/PENNETTE

1 KG/2.2 LB PEELED
  TOMATOES

150 G/6 OZ FRESH

  MOZZARELLA CHEESE,
  CUBED

100 G/4 OZ GRATED
  PARMESAN CHEESE

4 TABLESPOONS OLIVE OIL

BASIL

In a large saucepan, combine the tomatoes, olive oil, basil and a pinch of salt; cook for 20 minutes over a high flame.

Cook the pennette in boiling salted water until they are *al dente*, drain. Add the pasta to the tomato sauce and continue cooking over a medium flame, add the grated parmesan, the mozzarella and a few basil leaves.

Mix well, remove from the stove as soon as the mozzarella starts to melt. Serve immediately.

In Neapolitan dialect "sciué sciué" means something very, very simple.

SEDANI BELLA NAPOLI

400 G/14 OZ SEDANI
300 G/12 OZ LEAN LAMB OR PORK
180 G/7 OZ ROLLED BACON
120 G/5 OZ PEPPERONI SAUSAGE
200 G/8 OZ RICOTTA CHEESE
TOMATO SAUCE
1 CARROT
1 STALK CELERY
1 ONION
2 CLOVES GARLIC
ROSEMARY
RED HOT PEPPER
DRY WHITE WINE
VEGETABLE BROTH
OLIVE OIL

The generous amount of ingredients make this an ideal one-dish meal. It is an old holiday recipe. To guarantee its success, you need good, thick tomato sauce.

Clean the lamb and peel the sausages; put the meat into the blender and chop finely. Clean the carrot, onion and celery, chop finely with the garlic and rosemary. Sauté the vegetables in saucepan with 4-5 tablespoons olive oil.

Add the ground meats and brown slowly; add half a glass of white wine and let it evaporate.

Add 1 glass tomato sauce (if the sauce is not thick, add 1 cupful), a dash of salt and 1 or 2 red hot peppers.

Simmer for 1 hour, adding broth as needed.

Cook the sedani in boiling salted water until they are *al dente*, drain.

Put the pasta into the saucepan and top with the boiling hot sauce, turn off the flame. Add the ricotta, no other cheese is needed, mix and garnish with sprigs of rosemary. Rich and delicious!

There is another typically Neapolitan way of preparing sedani. Cook the sedani in boiling salted water until they are al dente, *drain. Put the pasta into an oven-dish and top with tomato sauce, a mozzarella cut into cubes, a handful of capers, anchovy fillets, oregano, basil, a pinch of salt and a dash of pepper. Smooth it down and then top with another mozzarella cut into medium-thick slices. Put the dish into the oven and light the grill. After about 10 minutes the top layer of mozzarella will start to melt and brown, remove from the oven and serve hot with a squiggle of olive oil, and, if you, garnish with fresh basil.*

TORTIGLIONI ALLE VONGOLE VERACI
TORTIGLIONI WITH CLAMS

350 G/12 OZ WHOLE WHEAT
   TORTIGLIONI

1 KG/2.2 LB CLAMS

1 CLOVE GARLIC, CRUSHED

2 GREEN ONIONS

DRY WHITE WINE

OLIVE OIL

If you buy the clams the night before you use them, or early in the morning, to keep them fresh wrap them in a wet dish towel and put them in the coolest part of your refrigerator, but not the freezer.

The best way to eliminate the sand in the clams is to soak them in lightly salted water. Place a dish, upside down in the bottom of the bowl with the salted water. As if by magic, the sand from the clams will collect under the dish. Change water 2 or 3 times until there is no trace of sand. Since most clams come from "farms", the sand is finer than normal sea sand and you may need to change the water more than 3 times, but it is well worth the effort. Discard the dead clams, the ones that don't open partly in the clean water, and obviously those that don't open when heated. Scoundrels!!

Clean and slice the onions. Put the rinsed clams into a pan with a little olive oil and the garlic. Heat over a high flame so they open, douse with half a glass of white wine and cook until the wine evaporates.

Turn off the flame, remove the clams (set them aside and keep them hot), and the garlic. You may have to strain the liquid through cheesecloth if the clams were not perfectly rinsed.

Cook the tortiglioni in boiling salted water until they are *al dente*. Put them in the pan with the liquid from the clams and cook over a high flame for a few minutes. Turn off the flame, add the sliced onions and mix. Add the clams in their open shells and serve. This is a fragrant and original dish, but remember, no cheese, please!

TUBETTI CON CACIO E UOVA
TUBETTI WITH CHEESE AND EGGS

400 G/14 OZ TUBETTI

3 EGGS BEATEN

100 G/4 OZ BUTTER

GRATED PARMESAN CHEESE

PARSLEY, CHOPPED

Cook the tubetti in boiling salted water until they are *al dente*, drain.

Melt the butter in a medium size skillet, add the beaten eggs, a pinch of salt, the tubetti, grated parmesan cheese and a dash of pepper. Mix well.

Cook over a very low flame until the eggs start to set, stir again, top with a sprinkling of parsley and serve hot.

ZITI AL RAGÙ CLASSICO
ZITI WITH CLASSIC NEAPOLITAN MEAT SAUCE

400 G/ 14 OZ ZITI

NEAPOLITAN MEAT SAUCE, SEE PAGE 65

GRATED PARMESAN CHEESE

For this dish use the classic Neapolitan meat sauce on page 65. Cook the ziti in boiling salted water until they are *al dente*, drain. Pour the ziti into a large serving bowl, top with the sauce (see page 65), mix well and serve immediately with grated parmesan cheese on the side.

CANNELLONI ALLA NAPOLETANA
NEAPOLITAN CANNELLONI

12 SQUARES OF EGG PASTA, ABOUT 12 CM ON A SIDE

MEAT SAUCE, SEE PAGE 67

100 G/4 OZ HAM, CHOPPED

200 G/8 OZ FRESH MOZZARELLA CHEESE, CUBED

300 G/12 OZ RICOTTA CHEESE

2 EGGS

100 G/4 OZ GRATED PARMESAN CHEESE

OLIVE OIL

BASIL

In a large bowl combine the eggs and ricotta cheese, mix well until creamy. Add the mozzarella, ham and parmesan continue mixing and add a tablespoon of the meat sauce, that is described on page 67.

Cook a few sheets of at a time pasta in boiling salted water with a squiggle of olive oil (the oil keeps the sheets of pasta from sticking together). The pasta for this recipe measures about 12 cm (4 in.) on a side.

Remove the squares well then are half done and place them on a clean cloth. Put a tablespoon of the sauce mixture in the middle of each and roll up.

Spread a generous amount of sauce in a baking dish, arrange the cannelloni in one layer and top with lots of meat sauce and grated parmesan cheese. Cover and bake at 180°C/350°F for 15 minutes; uncover and bake for another 10 minutes until slightly browned.

Garnish with basil leaves and serve.

CASATIELLO

500 G/1 LB FLOUR

200 G/8 OZ LARD

40G YEAST

6 EGGS, HARD-BOILED

2 TABLESPOONS GRATED
   PARMESAN CHEESE

1 TABLESPOON GRATED
   PECORINO CHEESE

Casatiello is similar to tortano in some ways. It is traditional Easter Sunday dish.

Combine the flour, yeast, a bit of the lard and a pinch of salt. Moisten with a little water and knead until soft. Cover the dough with a cloth and let it rise for about 2 hours. Knead again and roll out to a thickness of 1 cm (¹/₂ inch).

Grease a pan with the lard, sprinkle with the grated cheese and add a dash of pepper.

Fold the dough in half and knead. Repeat 3 times. Take a fistful of the dough and set it aside to rise. Roll up the rest of the dough, put it into a tube pan greased with lard and let it rise for about 3 hours.

Take the bit of dough you had set aside, roll it out and cut it into little "sticks". Push the shelled, hard-boiled eggs into the dough evenly spaced. To keep them steady, put two sticks of the dough, forming a cross, over each. Bake at 170°C/345°F for 1 hour until golden. Cool and remove from the pan. Casatiello, like tortano, can be stored for some time.

LASAGNE DI CARNEVALE

LASAGNA FOR MARDI GRAS

INGREDIENTS FOR 8

700 G/ 1 ³/₄ LB LASAGNA
    NOODLES

MEAT SAUCE, SEE PAGE 67

250 G/8 OZ CHOPPED BEEF

8 CERVELLATINE SAUSAGES

100 G/4 OZ STALE BREAD

400 G/14 OZ FRESH
    MOZZARELLA CHEESE,

1 KG/2.2 LB RICOTTA CHEESE

1 EGG

MILK

100 G/4 OZ GRATED
    PARMESAN CHEESE

VEGETABLE OIL

OLIVE OIL

Prepare the meat sauce according to the recipe on page 67. Soak the bread in milk, squeeze out well and add it to the chopped meat along with the grated parmesan cheese, the egg and a pinch of salt. Blend well, and shape into tiny meatballs. Fry the meatballs in hot vegetable oil and then drain on a paper towel.

Cook the cervellatine sausages, then slice thinly.

In a mixing bowl combine the ricotta cheese with a little lukewarm water, mix until creamy, flavor with a tablespoon of meat sauce. Pour the rest of the sauce into a saucepan with the cervellatine and meatballs, and cook for a few minutes.

Cook the lasagna noodles in boiling salted water with a squiggle of olive oil to keep them from sticking together, drain and lay them out on a clean cloth to dry.

Lightly grease a baking dish with a little sauce, make a first layer of noodles, overlapping slightly, like roof shingles, spread the ricotta mixture over them, sprinkle with grated parmesan cheese and a little mozzarella, top with the meat sauce, and repeat these layers until you have used all the noodles.

Bake at 180°C/350°F until a golden crust has formed. Remove from the oven and wait about 20 minutes before serving.

LASAGNE VESUVIO
LASAGNA MT. VESUVIUS

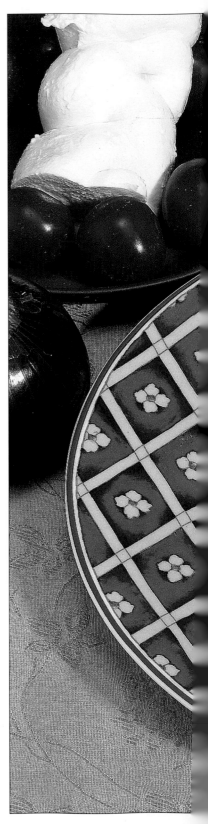

300 G/12 OZ FLOUR

6 EGGS

1 FRESH MOZZARELLA, SLICED

OLIVE OIL

OREGANO

BASIL

FOR THE SAUCE:

400 G/TOMATO PURÉE

1 CARROT, CHOPPED

1 ONION, CHOPPED

1 STALK CELERY, CHOPPED

OLIVE OIL

2-3 CLOVES GARLIC

1 SHALLOT, CHOPPED

Combine the flour and 3 eggs to make a dough. Set it aside.

In a saucepan gently sauté 1 clove of garlic in olive oil, remove the garlic and add the tomato pure, carrot, onion, celery, shallot, the remaining raw garlic, and a pinch of coarse salt. Add a tablespoon of olive oil, cover and cook slowly for 15 minutes. Turn off the flame, add 3-4 fresh basil leaves. Set aside uncovered to cool, then put the sauce through a food mill.

Roll out the dough and cut it into 8 x 14 cm rectangles.

Cook your homemade lasagna noodles in boiling salted water with a squiggle of olive oil, remove with a skimmer, and put on a clean cloth to dry.

Beat 3 eggs in a bowl.

Butter a baking dish and make a layer of lasagna noodles and cover them with the tomato sauce and little of the beaten eggs; place a few slices of mozzarella on top and sprinkle with oregano.

Keep on making layers until you have used all the noodles. End with the sauce and top with mozzarella slices. Bake at 180°C/350°F for 20 minutes. Remove, sprinkle with oregano and garnish with fresh basil leaves before serving.

GATTÓ DI PATATE
POTATO CAKE

1,250 KG/2 ½ LB POTATOES

150 G/6 OZ NEAPOLITAN
SALAMI, CHOPPED

250 G/8 OZ FRESH
MOZZARELLA
CHEESE, CUBED

4 EGGS

50 G/2 OZ GRATED PARMESAN
CHEESE

BREAD CRUMBS

100 G/4 OZ BUTTER

1 GLASS MILK

Hard-boil 2 eggs, peel and cut into wedges.

Boil the potatoes in their jackets, peel and put through a ricer.

In a mixing bowl combine 2 raw eggs, the butter, parmesan cheese and a dash of pepper, mix well adding milk a little at a time. Add the salami. Grease a baking dish with butter and sprinkle with bread crumbs, spread half the potato mixture and smooth it well.

Top with the egg wedges and the mozzarella cheese, cover with the remaining potato mixture and smooth the surface.

Top with a dusting of bread crumbs and dabs of butter and bake at 180°C/350°F until a golden crust is formed.

MACCHERONI GRATINATI
MACARONI AU GRATIN

INGREDIENTS FOR 6

400 G/14 OZ MACARONI

150 G/6 OZ HAM, CUT UP

200 G/8 OZ FRESH MOZZARELLA CHEESE, CUT UP

100 G/4 OZ FLOUR

100 G/4 OZ BUTTER

100 G/4 OZ PARMESAN GRATED CHEESE

2 TABLESPOONS BREAD CRUMBS

1 LITER/1 QUART MILK

GRATED NUTMEG

Cook the macaroni in boiling salted water until they are *al dente*, drain.

While the pasta is cooking, in a saucepan melt the butter, add the flour, milk, a dash of nutmeg and a pinch of salt, cook over a low flame, stirring constantly until the sauce thickens.

In a mixing bowl combine the macaroni, the sauce, mozzarella and ham.

Butter a large baking dish and pour in the macaroni mixture, sprinkle with the bread crumbs and top with the freshly grated parmesan cheese.

Bake in a moderate oven for 20 minutes, until golden.

Migliaccio con i ciccioli (cicoli)
CORNMEAL CAKE WITH LARD AND CHEESE

INGREDIENTS FOR 6

150 G/6 OZ CICCIOLI
(CRISP PORK SCRAPS)

400 G/14 OZ CORNMEAL

300 G/12 OZ SAUSAGE

100 G/4 OZ GRATED PECORINO
CHEESE

100 G/4 OZ GRATED
PARMESAN CHEESE

BREAD CRUMBS

BUTTER

PARSLEY

1.5 L/1 ½ QUART WATER

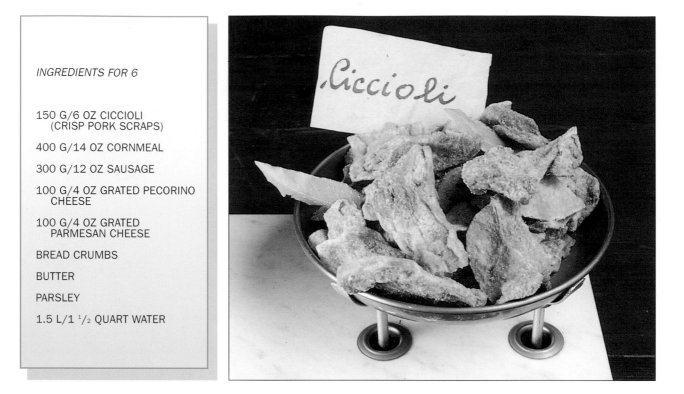

Puncture the sausages with a fork and brown in a skillet with a little butter. Drain and set them aside. Collect the sauce from the skillet and pour it into a large pot containing the salted water, bring to a boil, pour in the cornmeal, stir and cook for 40 minutes.

Slice the sausages. Then add the ciccioli, cheeses, sausage and parsley.

Butter a baking dish and sprinkle with bread crumbs, and fill with the rich cornmeal mixture.

Bake in a moderate oven for at least 30 minutes. Remove and wait 15 minutes before serving.

PERCIATELLI AL FORNO
OVEN-BAKED PERCIATELLI

INGREDIENTS FOR 6

400 G/14 PERCIATELLI

12 LARGE, RIPE TOMATOES

BREAD CRUMBS

2 DL / ½ CUP OLIVE OIL

2 CLOVES GARLIC

200 G/8 OZ BLACK OLIVES

100 G/4 OZ CAPERS

BASIL

Cut the tomatoes in half, remove the pulp and put it through a food mill, set aside the "empty" tomato halves.

In a skillet sauté the garlic in olive oil until slightly golden, add the tomato, capers and olives, cook slowly for 10 minutes.

Cook the pasta in boiling salted water for a few minutes, drain. Combine the pasta with the sauce. Grease a baking dish with olive oil, arrange 12 empty tomato halves in the dish, salt and fill with the dressed pasta, be sure to press down firmly. Perciatelli are thick and balky, so they obviously will overlap, and stick out from the tomatoes.

Cover each tomato with its matching half, garnish with a few fresh basil leaves and sprinkle with bread crumbs. Bake in a moderate over for 20 minutes.

PIZZA CON SCAROLA
PIZZA WITH ESCAROLE

BREAD DOUGH, SEE PAGE 73

6 BUNCHES OF ESCAROLE

1 EGG WHITE, SLIGHTLY BEATEN

FLOUR

2 TABLESPOONS OLIVE OIL

4 TABLESPOONS VEGETABLE OIL

2 CLOVES GARLIC

2 SALTED ANCHOVIES

100 G/4 OZ BLACK OLIVES

40 G/1 OZ CAPERS

50 G/2 OZ RAISINS

50 G/2 OZ PINE NUTS

10 DRIED FIGS

Prepare the bread dough according to the recipe on page 73.

Clean the escarole, scald in boiling water, drain, squeeze out the excess water.

In a medium size saucepan sauté the garlic in a little vegetable oil, add the escarole, and stir so that escarole absorbs the flavor.

Roll out the dough and make 2 round disks, one should be a little bigger.

Grease and flour a round cake pan, and line it the bigger disk of dough.

Put about half the escarole over the dough and sprinkle with half the raisins, pine nut, anchovies, olives and capers, cover the with remaining escarole and condiments.

Cover with the other disk of dough, press firmly to seal; pierce with a fork and brush with the beaten egg and top with a squiggle of olive oil.

Bake at 180°C/350°F until golden.

To enjoy the unusual combination of flavors in this pizza, let it cool a bit before serving.

SARTÙ DI RISO ROSSO
RED RICE SARTU

INGREDIENTS FOR 6

MEAT SAUCE, SEE PAGE 67
  DOUBLE THE RECIPE

250 G/8 OZ CHOPPED BEEF

8 CERVELLATINE SAUSAGES

100 G/4 OZ BACON, FINELY
  CHOPPED

350 G/12 OZ FRESH
  MOZZARELLA CHEESE

75 G STALE BREAD

450 G/1 LB RICE, PREFERABLY
  THE KIND RECOMMENDED
  FOR RISOTTO

500 G/1 LB GREEN PEAS

5 EGGS

2 HARD-BOILED EGGS

75 G GRATED PARMESAN
  CHEESE

BREAD CRUMBS

BUTTER

150 G/6 OZ OLIVE OIL

PARSLEY, CHOPPED

1 ONION, FINELY CHOPPED

WHITE WINE

This is a rather complex dish, that requires several steps in parallel. First prepare the meat sauce according to the recipe on page 67, doubling the quantities.

While the sauce is cooking, combine the chopped meat, stale bread, parsley and 2 raw eggs. Shape into meatballs, and fry immediately. Drain on paper towels.

In a skillet, sauté the cervellatine sausages and slice.

In a big skillet gently sauté the chopped bacon and onion, add the cervellatine, the meatballs, peas and a generous amount of meat sauce, dilute with a little white wine, cook covered over a very low flame.

Cut the hard-boiled eggs into wedges.

Beat the raw eggs with a pinch of salt, dash of pepper and a sprinkling of parmesan cheese.

Remove a few tablespoons of sauce from the pan and set aside. Pour the rice into the sauce and cook for 10 minutes, stirring constantly so that it does not stick.

Pour the cooked rice and sauce into a bowl to cool, add the beaten eggs and stir until thoroughly blended.

Butter a baking dish and sprinkle with bread crumbs. Take about one third of the rice mixture and put in the baking dish.

Cover with meat sauce, a few of the egg wedges and some of the mozzarella; repeat so that you end with a third and final layer of rice, sprinkle with bread crumbs and a few dots of butter.

Bake in a hot oven until evenly golden. Remove and let cool, then turn the sartu onto a platter and serve with the meat sauce you had put aside.

RISOTTO ALLA LUISELLA

INGREDIENTS FOR 6

400 G/14 OZ RICE

500 G/1 LB EELS

1 GLASS TOMATO SAUCE

OLIVE OIL

1 CLOVE GARLIC

1 ONION, THINLY SLICED

$^1/_2$ GLASS WHITE WINE

BROTH

Clean and wash the eels, skin and cut into pieces.
In a skillet sauté the onion and garlic in olive oil, add the eel. Add a little of the white wine, cook until it evaporates, and repeat until you have used it all.
Add the tomato sauce, salt to taste, and add a dash of pepper, cook for at least 15 minutes.
Add the rice and cook, adding a little broth now and then as cooking liquid for the rice.

TAGLIATELLE GRATINATE
TAGLIATELLE AU GRATIN

430 G/15 OZ FLOUR

7 EGGS

0.5 L/1 PT MILK

GRATED PARMESAN CHEESE

80 G/3 OZ BUTTER

OLIVE OIL

GRATED NUTMEG

Make your own tagliatelle noodles, by combining 400 g/14 oz. flour and 4 eggs, mix well and set aside for 30 minutes.
In a blender combine 30 g/1 oz flour, 2 tablespoons of grated parmesan cheese, the milk, a dash each of salt, pepper and grated nutmeg, and 50 g/2 oz melted butter.
Put the mixture into a saucepan and cook, stirring continuously until it thickens.
Remove from the stove and let cool. Separate the remaining 3 eggs and beat the whites until stiff; beat the yolks. First add the yolks to the mixture in the saucepan and then fold in the whites.
Roll out the dough, and cut it into 1 cm ($^1/_2$ inch) wide noodles.
Cook the noodles in boiling salted water with a few drops of olive oil to keep them from sticking. Drain and place into a buttered

baking dish, top with the milk and egg mixture and a generous sprinkling of grated parmesan cheese. Bake at 200°C/390°F for 10 minutes.

TIMBALLO PARTENOPE
NEAPOLITAN TIMBALE

300 G/12 OZ FLOUR

3 EGGS

300 G/12 OZ SPINACH

GRATED PARMESAN CHEESE

30 G/1 OZ BUTTER

OLIVE OIL

FILLING:

1 CUP MEAT SAUCE

400 G/14 OZ RICOTTA CHEESE

1 FRESH MOZZARELLA

2 HARD-BOILED EGGS

2 SAUSAGES

This exquisite timbale requires a good meat sauce, preferably one that is flavored with a little chopped red hot pepper.

Wash and cook the spinach, drain well and chop.

Combined the flour, eggs and chopped spinach to make the dough and set aside for 30 minutes.

Skin the sausages, crumble them into a skillet with a little water and brown.

Drain, and in the blender combine with the ricotta cheese, the meat sauce and dash of salt and pepper.

Slice the mozzarella and the hard-boiled eggs. Roll out the dough and cut 8 x 14 cm rectangles. Cook the pasta for about 6 minutes in boiling salted water with a few drops of olive oil to prevent sticking. Remove with a skimmer and lay the rectangles on a clean cry cloth.

Butter an oven dish and place a layer of the pasta rectangles, top with a little filling, and mozzarella and egg slices. Make another layer and repeat, ending with a layer of filling.

Sprinkle with grated parmesan cheese and bake at 200°C/390°F for 10 minutes.

TORTANO

500 G/1 LB FLOUR

300 G/12 OZ NEAPOLITAN
SALAMI, CUBED

150 G/6 OZ LARD

40 G/1-2 OZ YEAST

2 HARD-BOILED EGGS, SLICED

2 TABLESPOONS GRATED
PARMESAN CHEESE

2 TABLESPOONS GRATED
PECORINO CHEESE

Combine the flour, yeast, a little of the lard and a pinch of salt, moisten with water and mix until the dough becomes elastic.

Cover with a cloth and set aside to rise for about 2 hours.

Sprinkle your work table with flour, knead the dough and add the cheeses and a dash or two of pepper, knead well and roll out the dough to a thickness of 0.5 cm (¼ inch). Spread with some lard, and scatter the salami cubes and egg slices over and roll it up. Grease a tube pan with lard and place the roll of dough into, making sure that the two ends meet, press them firmly together to seal. Set aside for at least 3 hours so that it will rise again.

Bake at 170°C/345°F for 1 hour.

Cool thoroughly then turn out from the pan.

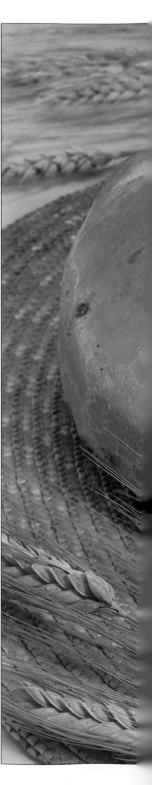

Tortano is a typical savory cake that is very dear to Neapolitan tradition. One of its outstanding features is that it will keep perfectly for several days.

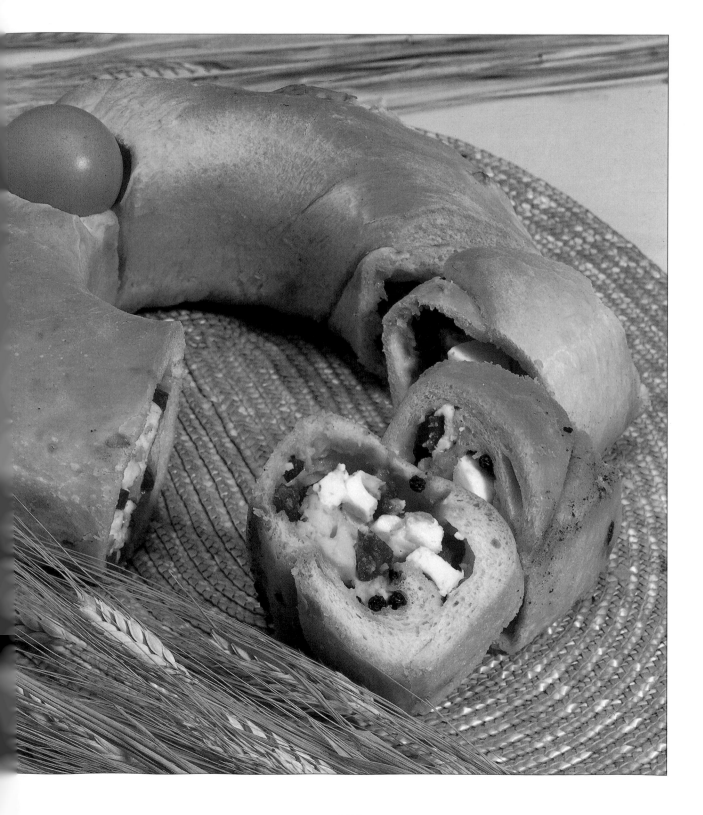

FISH AND SEAFOOD

ALICI IN TORTIERA
ANCHOVIES IN TORTIERA

800 G/1 ¾ LB FRESH
ANCHOVIES

BREAD CRUMBS

1 DL/ ½ CUP OLIVE OIL

2 TABLESPOONS VINEGAR

2 CLOVES GARLIC

1 SPRIG PARSLEY

OREGANO

Chop the garlic and parsley together. Clean the anchovies, removing the backbones.

Put the anchovies into a medium size skillet greased with little olive oil, sprinkle with the chopped garlic and parsley, bread crumbs and a dash of salt.

Add some more olive oil then cook covered for a few minutes, over a low flame. Add the vinegar and a pinch of oregano and continue cooking over a high flame.

You can also cook these anchovies in the oven if you prefer.

BACCALÀ IN CASSUOLA
STEWED CODFISH

1 KG/2.2 LB SALTED CODFISH

TOMATO PUREE

FLOUR

2 TABLESPOONS OLIVE OIL

VEGETABLE OIL

GARLIC

50 G/2 OZ BLACK OLIVES

25 G/1 OZ SALTED CAPERS

30 G/1 OZ PINE NUTS

50 G/2 OZ RAISINS

Flavor the tomato puree with the garlic and olive oil. Rinse and skin the codfish. Cut it into medium size pieces and coat them with flour. Fry the codfish in vegetable oil. Fry a few pieces at a time so they can brown evenly.

Drain on paper towels.

Put the fried codfish in a skillet that is large to hold it all in a single layer, cover with the tomato sauce and add the olives, capers, pine nuts and raisins.

Cook covered for 30 minutes, until the sauce thickens. Salt to taste before serving.

CALAMARI IMBOTTITI
STUFFED SQUID

8 LARGE SQUID

500 G/1 LB TOMATO PUREE

80 G/3 OZ BREAD CRUMBS

1 DL/ ¹/₂ CUP OLIVE OIL

3 CLOVES GARLIC

1 SPRIG PARSLEY, CHOPPED

80 G/3 OZ PITTED BLACK
     OLIVES

40 G/1 OZ SALTED CAPERS

Chop the garlic, capers and olives. Clean the squid. Removing the fins and tentacles, chop them and sauté them in a skillet.

Add a little of the bread crumbs and the garlic, capers and olive mixture and combine thoroughly. Add a sprinkling of chopped parsley and salt to taste, set aside to cool.

Stuff the squid with the mixture and sew them closed. Place the stuffed squid in a skillet, top with the tomato pure and add a clove of garlic and a squiggle of olive oil.

Cook covered over a moderate flame for about 1 hour.

Garnish with chopped parsley just before serving.

CAPITONE AL FORNO
OVEN-BAKED EEL

3 EEL

12 BAY LEAVES

1 KG/2.2 LB COARSE SALT

For Neapolitans this is a traditional dish for Christmas and New Year's. The number of capitone is approximate, the important thing is to have 12 good-sized pieces.

Clean the fish, cut off the heads and tails, cut them into 10 cm (4 inch) pieces. Soak the pieces in salted water for several hours, and be sure to change the water at least twice.
Remove the pieces one at a time, drain and dry them and put a bay leaf into each.
Heat the oven and put the fish under the hot grill for 10 to 15 minutes.

CAPITONE ALLA MARINARA
EEL ALLA MARINARA

INGREDIENTS FOR 6

1 KG/2.2 LB EEL

400 G/14 OZ TOMATOES

OLIVE OIL

2 CLOVES GARLIC, CHOPPED

PARSLEY, CHOPPED

Clean the eel carefully, cut it into pieces and put the pieces into a skillet with olive oil, the garlic, salt, pepper and tomatoes.
Cook over a high flame for 30 minutes. Remove from the stove and flavor with a handful of chopped parsley.

This same recipe is ideal for cooking other types of eel too.

CAPITONE FRITTO
FRIED EEL

12 PIECES OF EEL
FLOUR
VEGETABLE OIL

Coat the eel in flour and fry in hot vegetable oil until golden. Remove one at a time and drain on paper towels. You may want to add a pinch or two of salt.

Neapolitan tradition calls for this dish to be served with the hearty salad on page 158, but any salad is fine as long as it is dressed with oil and vinegar.

"CECENIELLI" FRITTI IN PASTELLA
BATTER FRIED "WHITEBAIT"

600 G/21 OZ "WHITEBAIT" OR SMALL FISH FOR FRYING
250 G/8 OZ FLOUR
1 CUBE BREWER'S YEAST
VEGETABLE OIL
WATER
LEMON

Dissolve the yeast in a glass of lukewarm water.
Combine the flour and salt in a bowl and add the water with the dissolved yeast.
Blend and keep on adding lukewarm water until the batter is creamy.
Mix the batter for another 10 minutes and then cover the bowl with a wool cloth and set it aside to rise for 1 hour.
When it has risen, add the "whitebait".
Whitebait is very delicate, so you must be careful not to crush

them as you stir them in the batter. Drop one table spoon of batter into the hot oil at a time. As soon as the batter touches the oil it will puff out. Fry until golden.

Use a skimmer to remove the fried patties and drain on paper towels. Salt to taste and garnish with lemon slices.

Serve hot.

PESCE ALL'ACQUA PAZZA

SEA BASS ALL'ACQUA PAZZA

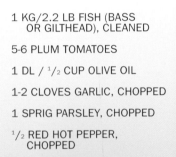

1 KG/2.2 LB FISH (BASS OR GILTHEAD), CLEANED

5-6 PLUM TOMATOES

1 DL / $^{1}/_{2}$ CUP OLIVE OIL

1-2 CLOVES GARLIC, CHOPPED

1 SPRIG PARSLEY, CHOPPED

$^{1}/_{2}$ RED HOT PEPPER, CHOPPED

Place the fish in a large skillet. Cut the tomatoes in half and put them in the skillet along with the garlic, parsley and red hot pepper. Cover with aluminum foil so that no steam can escape and cook over a low flame.

When the fish is tender, salt to taste.

Place the fish on a serving platter and flavor with the cooking liquid.

POLPI ALLA LUCIANA
OCTOPUS ALLA LUCIANA

4-5 SMALL OCTOPUS

1 DL/ 1/2 CUP OLIVE OIL

1 CLOVE GARLIC

1 SPRIG PARSLEY

LEMON

Clean the octopus carefully. Boil them into a large terra-cotta pot that closes tightly, add a glass of salt water to the pot (sea water would be preferable, but is not always available).

Boiling octopus takes about 30-45 minutes, depending on their size. When they are done, drain.

Before serving, cut them into pieces and garnish with olive oil, pepper, lemon, parsley and a little garlic.

Chopped, raw celery adds a special touch of flavor.

TOTANI E PATATE
SQUID AND POTATOES

1 KG/2.2 LB SQUID

700 G/1 ³/₄ LB POTATOES

500 G/1 LB PEELED TOMATOES

4 TABLESPOONS OLIVE OIL

2 CLOVES GARLIC

¹/₂ GLASS WHITE WINE

PARSLEY

RED HOT PEPPER

Clean, wash and cut up the squid. Place them in a large saucepan and add a little garlic, olive oil and red hot pepper; cook over a high flame.

The heat will make the squid release their liquid, it is important to continue cooking until this occurs, add white wine occasionally as they cook.

Peel the potatoes and cut them into medium size pieces, and soak them in fresh water. Drain and dry the potatoes, then along with the tomatoes and a dash of salt add them to the squid which should be cooking for a while already.

Stir and then cook covered over a medium flame for about 45 minutes.

Serve the squid while they are still warm, garnish with chopped parsley if you like.

TRIGLIE ALLA PESCATORA
MULLET ALLA PESCATORA

4 MULLET, WEIGHING ABOUT
  200 G/8 OZ EACH

1 DL/ ½ CUP OLIVE OIL

3 CLOVES GARLIC, FINELY
  CHOPPED

PARSLEY, CHOPPED

JUICE OF 2 LEMONS

Clean the fish carefully and remove their insides, wash them and let them drain thoroughly.

In a bowl prepare a marinade by combining the olive oil, garlic, parsley, lemon juice, salt and pepper.

Coat the fish with the sauce and place them under a hot grill, cook for 3 minutes on each side.

TRIGLIE AL CARTOCCIO
MULLET BAKED IN FOIL

4 MULLET, WEIGHING ABOUT
   300 G/12 OZ EACH

4 TABLESPOONS BREAD
   CRUMBS

1 DL/ $^1/_2$ CUP OLIVE OIL

$^1/_2$ MEDIUM CLOVE GARLIC

1 SPRIG PARSLEY

OREGANO

JUICE OF $^1/_2$ LEMON

Clean the mullet, remove the scales, rinse and drain. Place each fish on a piece of aluminum foil large enough to wrap around and close.

Heat the oil and bread crumbs in a skillet, stirring constantly. When they are golden, remove the skillet from the stove and pour on the lemon juice, the garlic, a pinch of oregano and a sprinkling of parsley.

Mix well and brush over each fish.

For best results, you should use mullet from rocky coasts, they are harder to come by, but are better than those from sandy shores.

Coat an oven dish with a little olive oil, close the wrappers, place them side by side in the dish and bake at 200°C/390°F for at least 20 minutes.

MEATS

AGNELLO IN FRICASSEA
LAMB FRICASSEE

1.5 KG/3 LB LAMB

400 G/15 OZ SHELLED PEAS

50 G/2 OZ LARD

50 G/2 OZ GRATED PARMESAN
   CHEESE

3 EGGS

3 TABLESPOONS OLIVE OIL

PARSLEY, CHOPPED

2 ONIONS, SLICED

1 GLASS WHITE WINE

JUICE OF 1 LEMON

Rinse and slice the meat. Beat the eggs slightly with the parmesan cheese, parsley and a pinch of salt, set aside.

Heat the condiments in a medium saucepan, and then brown 2 slices of meat at a time, remove and set aside on a plate.

In the sauce that forms, cook the onions over a low flame, adding a little water if they tend to stick. When they are done, take off a tablespoon of onion and a little sauce, and put in another saucepan with the peas.

Cook the peas slowly, adding water now and then.

Put the meat back into the first pan, add the wine and cook thoroughly.

Add the peas and the beaten egg mixture. Mix and cook for a few more minutes, add the lemon juice, wait until it evaporates then serve.

BRACIOLE AL RAGÙ
CUTLETS IN MEAT SAUCE

12 SLICES OF BEEF OR PORK

200 G/8 OZ BACON

150 G/6 OZ GRATED
   PARMESAN AND PECORINO
   CHEESE

140 G/6 OZ TOMATO
   CONCENTRATE

500 G/1 LB TOMATO PUREE

4 TABLESPOONS OLIVE OIL

2 CLOVES GARLIC

1 GLASS RED WINE

1 ONION, SLICED

2 SPRIGS PARSLEY

150 G/6 OZ RAISINS AND PINE
   NUTS

The sauce you obtain from this recipe is also an excellent condiment for thick pasta. If you plan on using it for pasta, be sure to increase the quantities of tomato puree and tomato concentrate.

Trim and pound the meat. Chop the bacon, garlic and parsley together. Sprinkle each slice of meat with the parmesan and pecorino cheeses, then, in middle of each put a spoonful of the bacon mixture, pine nuts and raisins.

Roll up each slice and tie it so that the filling does not fall out.

Brown them in a skillet with olive oil and the onion, add the tomato puree and concentrate, and the red wine.

The tomato should become creamy, you may need to add a little salted water.

Cook for 60 to 90 minutes.

When the meat is tender, remove it from the skillet and put it on a plate. Let the sauce simmer, then untie the string and put the meat back into the sauce, heat and serve hot.

BRACIOLE DI COTICA DI MAIALE
PORK RIND CUTLETS

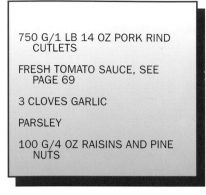

750 G/1 LB 14 OZ PORK RIND CUTLETS

FRESH TOMATO SAUCE, SEE PAGE 69

3 CLOVES GARLIC

PARSLEY

100 G/4 OZ RAISINS AND PINE NUTS

Prepare your fresh tomato sauce according to the recipe on page 69. Chop the parsley and garlic together.

Sear the pork rind to remove any bristles, rinse and dip into boiling water for a minute or two. This will remove excess fat and make the meat tender. Set aside to cool and dry.

When the meat is cool, cut it into medium size rectangles. Place a pinch of the garlic and parsley mixture and raisins and pine nuts on each, salt lightly, roll them up and tie. Put the meat rolls into a saucepan with the tomato sauce and cook covered over a medium flame. Add a little hot water if it tends to dry or stick. Cook for about 3 hours, until tender. Serve hot, topped with the sauce.

BRACIOLONE DI VITELLO
ROLLED SHOULDER OF VEAL

INGREDIENTS FOR 6

1 KG/2.2 LB VEAL SHOULDER, IN ONE THICK SLICE

100 G/4 OZ BACON, SLICED

1 EGG

30 G/1 OZ BUTTER

1 TABLESPOON GRATED PARMESAN CHEESE

1 TABLESPOON OLIVE OIL

1 SPRIG PARSLEY, CHOPPED

1 STALK CELERY, CHOPPED

1 ONION, CHOPPED

1 CARROT, CHOPPED

$^{1}/_{2}$ GLASS WHITE WINE

2 DL/1 CUP BROTH

Trim the meat and pound to tenderize. Make an omelet using the egg, grated parmesan cheese, a little chopped parsley and salt.

Place the hot omelet and the sliced bacon on top of the meat. Roll it up and tie the ends.

Place it in a skillet with the butter, olive oil and the chopped vegetables. Cook over a low flame and turn the meat occasionally to keep it from burning. Add the wine, when it has evaporated add the broth.

When the meat is tender remove it from the skillet, remove the string and slice.

Top with the cooking sauce and serve.

COSCIOTTO D'AGNELLO ALLA LISETTA
LEG OF LAMB ALLA LISETTA

1 LEG OF LAMB, BONED

300 G/12 OZ LB SAUSAGES

STALE BREAD, WITHOUT THE
    CRUST

1 EGG

1 GLASS MILK

GRATED PARMESAN CHEESE

OLIVE OIL

GRATED NUTMEG

1 GLASS WHITE WINE

Soak the bread in the milk, and then squeeze it out. Skin the sausages, and crumble them together with the bread. Add the egg, parmesan cheese, a dash each of nutmeg, salt and pepper and mix well.

Fill the leg of lamb with the mixture, tie it and place it in an pan with the olive oil. Brown it slowly, turning it so that it cooks evenly. Add a pinch or two of salt and the white wine. Bake in a moderate oven until tender.

Cut thick slices and serve.

CAPRETTO ALLA NAPOLETANA
NEAPOLITAN KID

INGREDIENTS FOR 6

2 KG/4.4 LB KID

800 G /1¹/₂ LB GREEN PEAS

4 EGGS

50 G/2 OZ GRATED PARMESAN
    CHEESE

OLIVE OIL

1 ONION, SLICED

1 LEMON

WATER

Cook the peas. Rinse and dry the meat, then cut it into chunks.

Sauté the onion in a little olive oil until tender. Add the meat and cook over a medium to low flame, add water as needed to keep it from drying and salt to taste.

When the meat is half done, add the peas.

In a bowl, beat the eggs with the parmesan cheese, salt and a dash of pepper. Pour the egg mixture into the pan with the meat and peas and stir quickly so that the egg cooks evenly.

Squeeze the juice of 1 lemon over it all before serving.

CARNE ALLA PIZZAIOLA
PORK CHOPS ALLA PIZZAIOLA

4 PORK CHOPS

TOMATO SAUCE, SEE PAGE 67

OREGANO

Bone the pork chops and brown them in a skillet. When the chops are evenly browned, pour on the tomato sauce (see recipe on page 67) and lower the flame. Cook slowly for a few minutes, turning the meat so it can absorb all the flavor of the sauce. Serve hot, with a sprinkling of oregano.

CONIGLIO ALL'ISCHITANA
RABBIT ISCHIA STYLE

1 RABBIT

8 SMALL TOMATOES

1 DL/ $^{1}/_{2}$ CUP OLIVE OIL

6 CLOVES GARLIC

ROSEMARY

SAGE

CELERY

BAY LEAVES

HOT RED PEPPER

$^{1}/_{2}$ GLASS RED WINE,
      PREFERABLY FROM ISCHIA

Clean the rabbit, set the liver aside. Soak the rabbit in water for 30 minutes then dry it thoroughly. Cut the rabbit into pieces.

Chop the herbs together, and place in a large saucepan with the olive oil and unpeeled garlic cloves. Cook over a very low flame until the garlic is lightly browned; remove the garlic and herbs and set them aside.

Now, brown the rabbit, 2 pieces at a time in the flavored oil, remove and set aside.

When they are all browned, put them back into the pan, lower the flame and gradually add the red wine. Then add the herbs and garlic along with a little red hot pepper and the tomatoes. Cook covered, salt to taste. When the meat is tender, add the liver, cut into cubes and cook for 5 minutes.

MAIALE CON LE "PAPACCELLE"
PORK WITH PICKLED PEPPERS

4 PORK CHOPS

3 PEPPERS PICKLED IN VINEGAR

BUTTER

Grease a skillet with butter and cook the pork chops over a high flame, turning them frequently so they brown evenly. Remove the peppers from the vinegar, slice, and remove the seeds. When the meat is about half done, add the peppers and cook for 5 minutes; add salt a pepper to taste before serving.

GRANATINE ALLA SALSA DI POMODORO
MEAT PATTIES IN TOMATO SAUCE

400 G/14 OZ CHOPPED MEAT

200 G/8 OZ STALE BREAD, SOAKED AND SQUEEZED

TOMATO SAUCE, SEE PAGE 67

1 WHOLE EGG PLUS 1 YOLK

1 TABLESPOON GRATED PARMESAN CHEESE

BREAD CRUMBS

VEGETABLE OIL

BASIL

Prepare the tomato sauce according to the recipe on page 67 put it into a sauce boat and add a few fresh basil leaves for extra fragrance. Combine the meat, bread, egg and yolk, and cheese in a bowl and mix. Make oblong patties not more than 2 cm thick. Coat the patties with bread crumbs and fry in hot oil.

Drain on paper towels. Serve lukewarm with the tomato sauce on the side, that is truly the best condiment for these patties that are known as "granatine" in Neapolitan dialect.

POLLO ALLA SCARPARIELLO
CHICKEN ALLA SCARPARIELLO

INGREDIENTS FOR 6

1 CHICKEN

10 SMALL TOMATOES

OLIVE OIL

BASIL

1 ONION, SLICED

Clean and wash the chicken, dry it thoroughly and cut it into 8 pieces. Brown the chicken in a skillet with olive oil and a dash of pepper.

When it is evenly brown, add the tomatoes, cut in half, a little basil, the onion, a dash of pepper and salt to taste. Cover tightly and cook over a moderate flame until the chicken is tender. Serve hot.

POLPETTONE AL FORNO
MEAT LOAF

INGREDIENTS FOR 8

700 G/1 LB 12 OZ CHOPPED MEAT

100 G/4 OZ HAM

150 G/6 OZ BOLOGNA

150 G/6 OZ FRESH MOZZARELLA CHEESE, SLICED

250 G/STALE BREAD, SOAKED AND SQUEEZED

2 WHOLE EGGS + 2 YOLKS

2 HARD-BOILED EGGS, SHELLED

2 TABLESPOONS GRATED PARMESAN CHEESE

75 G/3 OZ BUTTER

FLOUR

PARSLEY, CHOPPED

In a large bowl combine the meat, bread, parmesan cheese, the 2 whole eggs, 2 yolks and a dash of pepper. When the mixture is compact, cover it with a cloth and set it aside for about 1 hour. Sprinkle a sheet of aluminum foil with flour, put the meat mixture on it and flatten it to form a rectangle. Cut the ends off the hard-boiled eggs, so that you can see the yolk.

Place the ham, bologna and cheese slices one on top of the other in the middle, then arrange the eggs end-to-end. Roll up the meat, press down the ends to seal and dredge in flour.

Grease an oven pan with butter, put in the meat and dot with butter.

Cover with aluminum foil and bake at 180°C/350° F for 30 minutes, remove the cover and continue baking for another 15 minutes.

Slice and serve.

SALTIMBOCCA ALLA SORRENTINA

500 G/1 LB VEAL RUMP, SLICED

70 G/3 OZ CURED HAM, SLICED

150 G/6 OZ FRESH MOZZARELLA CHEESE, SLICED

TOMATO SAUCE, SEE PAGE 68

FLOUR

2 TABLESPOONS GRATED PARMESAN CHEESE

50 G/2 OZ BUTTER

2 TABLESPOONS OLIVE OIL

Prepare the tomato concentrate sauce according to the recipe on page 68.

Trim the meat and pound the slices to tenderize.

Dredge the meat in flour and brown in a skillet with butter and olive oil.

Put the meat into an oven dish greased with butter, top each piece with a slice of ham and cheese, and the tomato sauce. Sprinkle with grated parmesan cheese.

Remove from the oven when the mozzarella has melted.

VEGETABLES

CAPONATA

4 DRY PIECES ROUND, WHOLE
    BREAD, "FRESELLE"

500 G/1 LB RIPE TOMATOES

1 DL/ ¹/₂ CUP OLIVE OIL

2 LARGE CLOVES GARLIC

5-6 BASIL LEAVES

OREGANO

Quickly moisten the freselle with water, then rub with garlic and salt to taste.

Place them in a large salad bowl, add the sliced tomatoes, oregano and chopped garlic.

Sprinkle generously with olive oil and mix well; wait about 30 minutes before serving.

This classic caponata can be enriched and varied according to your taste. There are several ingredients you can add such as anchovies, tuna fish, green or black olives, fresh celery, onion, and sliced hard-boiled egg, making it a tasty main dish.

"FRIARIELLI" SOFFRITTI
SAUTÉED TURNIP TOPS

1.5 KG/3 LB "TURNIP TOPS", UNCLEANED

1 DL/ 1/2 CUP OLIVE OIL

2 CLOVES GARLIC

HOT RED PEPPER

Wash and dry the greens.

In a skilled, sauté the garlic and a pinch of hot red pepper in olive oil, salt to cook. Add the greens, covered over a low flame, stirring occasionally. When they are nearly tender, uncover and continue cooking until the water released by the turnip tops has evaporated completely.

Sautéed turnip tops are an ideal side dish to serve with pork, especially chops, sausages and cervellatine.

INSALATA CAPRESE
CAPRI SALAD

1-3 TOMATOES

400 G/14 OZ FRESH MOZZARELLA CHEESE

OLIVE OIL

6-7 BASIL LEAVES

OREGANO

Cut the mozzarella into medium-thick slices.

Slice the tomatoes to about the same thickness.

Alternate the cheese and tomato slices on individual plates, garnish with basil leaves and season with a dash of salt and oregano, and extra virgin olive oil.

INSALATA DI RINFORZO
HEARTY SALAD

1 KG/2.2 LB CAULIFLOWER

1 PEPPER PICKLED IN VINEGAR

1 HARD-BOILED EGG

1 DL OLIVE OIL

1 GLASS STRONG VINEGAR

1 ANCHOVIES IN OLIVE OIL

200 G/8 OZ MIXED VEGETABLES
IN VINEGAR

70 G/3 OZ GREEN OLIVES

70 G/3 OZ BLACK OLIVES

COARSE SALT

Separate the cauliflower blossoms, wash and let dry. Cook the cauliflower in boiling salted water and remove while still firm. Cool immediately under cold running water so they maintain their consistency.

Put them into a large salad bowl and douse with vinegar; cover and set aside for 1 hour.

Add the olives, the vegetables preserved in vinegar, the anchovies, the pepper cut into strips, and the olive oil. Mix well, garnish with sliced hard-boiled egg.

Sprinkle with salt and let the salad sit for a few hours before serving.

INVOLTINI DI MELANZANE CON CARNE
STUFFED EGGPLANT

4 MEDIUM SIZE EGGPLANTS

200 G/8 OZ CHOPPED MEAT

150 G/6 OZ BREAD, SOAKED
IN MILK

GRATED PARMESAN CHEESE

1 EGG

0.5 L /2 CUPS TOMATO PUREE

VEGETABLE OIL

BASIL

GROUND NUTMEG

Carefully peel the eggplants, and slice them lengthwise. Fry the slices in hot oil until they golden.
Drain on paper towels.
In the meantime, combine the remaining ingredients and make little meatballs. Place one meatball on each slice of fried eggplant and roll up.
Put some of the tomato puree in an oven dish, put the eggplant rolls over the tomato and top with the grated parmesan cheese, more tomato puree and a few basil leaves. Bake in a moderate, preheated oven for about 15 minutes or until the tomato sauce starts to thicken.

Involtini di Peperoni
STUFFED PEPPERS

3 PEPPERS

100 G/4 OZ HAM

300 G/12 OZ FRESH MOZZARELLA CHEESE, CUT INTO SMALL PIECES

40 G/1 OZ GRATED PARMESAN CHEESE

3 SLICES WHITE BREAD

BREAD CRUMBS

1 EGG

OLIVE OIL

In a mixing bowl, combine the mozzarella cheese, ham, egg, crumbled white bread, and the parmesan cheese, blend well, salt to taste and add a dash of pepper.

Wash the peppers (yellow ones are best, if possible), grill them, remove the skins and seeds and cut into large slices.

Put about a tablespoon of the cheese mixture on each slice, and roll it up. Prepare an oven dish with high edges by coating with olive oil and sprinkling with bread crumbs, arrange the pepper rolls side by side and bake at 180°C/350°F for 10 minutes.

MELANZANE A BARCHETTA
EGGPLANT BOATS

4 EGGPLANTS

500 G/1 LB PEELED TOMATOES

BREAD CRUMBS

2-3 TABLESPOONS
    VEGETABLE OIL

1 CLOVE GARLIC, CRUSHED

100 G/4 OZ BLACK OLIVES

30 G/1 OZ SALTED CAPERS

BASIL

OREGANO

Cut the eggplants lengthwise, remove the pulp, chop and fry it immediately.

Remove the fried pulp from the skillet and set it aside to dry. In another skillet fry the empty skins, or "boats".

Combine the fried pulp with the garlic and tomatoes to make a sauce. Add the capers, pitted chopped olives, bread crumbs and flavor with a pinch of oregano.

Blend well, then fill each of the fried empty skins wit the mixture. Place the "boats" in an oven dish, garnish with fresh basil and bake for 20 minutes.

PEPERONI IN PADELLA COL POMODORO
SAUTÉED PEPPERS WITH TOMATO

1 KG/2.2 LB GREEN PEPPERS

350 G/13 OZ PEELED
    TOMATOES

VEGETABLE OIL

2 CLOVES GARLIC

Fry the peppers in hot oil and set them aside. Remove most of the oil, leave just enough to sauté the garlic, add the peeled tomatoes, cut into pieces. Cook for a few minutes, stirring continuously, salt to taste and put the peppers back to cook until they have absorbed the liquid and flavors.

Scarola imbottita
STUFFED ESCAROLE

8 HEADS ESCAROLE

100 G/4 OZ BREAD CRUMBS

2 DL/1 CUP OLIVE OIL

2 CLOVES GARLIC

2 ANCHOVIES

PARSLEY

100 G/4 OZ BLACK OLIVES

50 G/2 OZ CAPERS

30 G/1 OZ RAISINS

30 G/1 OZ PINE NUTS

COARSE SALT

Clean the anchovies, and rinse off the salt. Sauté the 2 cloves of garlic in a little olive oil until barely golden and remove them.

Add the chopped parsley, olives, capers, the anchovies, about 2/3 of the bread crumbs, pine nuts and raisins and stir to get an evenly blended mixture.

Prepare the escarole by removing the base and the tough outer leaves.

Wash thoroughly and then dip each one separately into boiling salted water for a few minutes. Set aside to dry.

When they are thoroughly drained, fill them with part of the mixture and tie the tops to prevent the filling from coming out.

Grease an oven dish with olive oil, place the stuffed escarole in the dish, sprinkle with bread crumbs and a little olive oil. Cover with aluminum foil and bake at 180°C/350°F for 15 minutes. Uncover and continue baking for another few minutes until the water evaporates.

Serve hot.

ZUCCHINE ALLA "SCAPECE"

1 KG/2 LB ZUCCHINI

4 TABLESPOONS OLIVE OIL

VINEGAR

2 CLOVES GARLIC

MINT LEAVES

OREGANO

HOT RED PEPPER

Wash and dry the zucchini. Slice thinly and boil in salted water with ½ a glass of vinegar.

Drain and cool slightly. Put the zucchini into a large bowl and flavor with oregano, mint, garlic, a pinch of ground hot red pepper, a generous amount of olive oil and a squiggle of vinegar.

Cover and refrigerate for 2 or 3 hours so the zucchini absorb all the flavors.

FRIED FOODS

ALGHE FRITTE
FRIED ALGAE

INGREDIENTS FOR 10

2-3 BUNCHES OF SEA ALGAE

300 G/12 OZ LB FLOUR

20 G/1 OZ YEAST

VEGETABLE OIL

WATER

Wash the algae, squeeze out excess water and set them aside to dry.

In the meantime, prepare the batter. Dissolve the yeast in a little lukewarm water, gradually add the flour and blend with a fork, keep on adding lukewarm water until you get a nice, thick batter. Salt, cover the bowl and set aside to rise for 1 hour. Add the algae and mix thoroughly but gently. Drop tablespoons of the batter into hot oil do not fry more than 4 tablespoons of batter at a time so that there will be room for it to puff up. Remove when evenly golden and drain on paper towels. Serve hot.

CROCCHETTE DI PATATE
POTATO CROQUETTES

INGREDIENTS FOR 10

1 KG/2.2 LB POTATOES

150 G/6 OZ AGED
  MOZZARELLA CHEESE

FLOUR

1 EGG + 2 YOLKS FOR
  THE MIXTURE

1 EGG + 2 WHITES FOR
  COATING

50 G/2 OZ BUTTER

100 G/4 OZ GRATED
  PARMESAN CHEESE

2 L/2 QUARTS VEGETABLE OIL

PARSLEY

Boil the potatoes in the jackets, pour off the water and dry them over a medium flame.

In a mixing bowl combine the parmesan cheese, butter, 1 whole egg and 2 yolks, a little chopped parsley, add the still-warm peeled and crushed potatoes. Mix well to form a puree. Sprinkle with salt and pepper and continue mixing. When it is homogeneous, wet your hands and make little cylinders, push a little cube of mozzarella into each one. Beat the egg and 2 whites together slightly. Dredge the croquettes in flour, dip into the beaten egg, roll in bread crumbs and fry in hot oil until golden. Serve hot.

FIORI DI ZUCCA FRITTI
FRIED ZUCCHINI BLOSSOMS

300 G/12 OZ ZUCCHINI
BLOSSOMS

BATTER, SEE PAGE 106

VEGETABLE OIL

Clean the zucchini blossoms: remove the pistil and the little, green outer petals.

Prepare the batter according to the recipe on page 166, for fried algae. Dip the blossoms into the batter until they are well coated. Remove them with a spoon and toss them into a frying pan filled with hot oil. Turn them gently so they brown evenly. Salt moderately and serve hot.

MOZZARELLA IN CARROZZA
FRIED MOZZARELLA

INGREDIENTS FOR 8

500 G/1 LB AGED
    MOZZARELLA CHEESE

3-4 EGGS

3-4 TABLESPOONS MILK

FLOUR

500 G/1 LB SLICED WHITE
    BREAD

VEGETABLE OIL

Beat the eggs in a bowl, salt moderately and add the milk. Remove the crust from the bread. Slice the mozzarella as thick as the bread slices and make sandwiches.
Dredge in flour, then dip into the egg and milk mixture (add milk as you go along so the mixture does not dry out). Fry in hot oil until golden, drain on paper towels and serve hot. A dash of freshly ground pepper will enhance the flavor.

PANZEROTTI

INGREDIENTS FOR 8-10

BREAD DOUGH, SEE PAGE 73

3 EGGS

100 G/4 OZ SMOKED
  PROVOLONE CHEESE

100 GS/4 OZ NEAPOLITAN

  SALAMI

70 G/3 OZ GRATED PARMESAN
  CHEESE

VEGETABLE OIL

PARSLEY

Prepare bread dough according to the recipe on page 73.

In a large bowl combine 2 whole eggs, 1 yolk, the parmesan cheese, chopped parsley and a dash of salt; beat gently. When the mixture is well blended, add the salami cut into small cubes, and the provolone cheese.

When the dough has risen, flour the work table and roll it out thinly. Use a glass to cut small disks, place a bit of the egg mixture in the middle of each and then fold in half, press the edges firmly to seal. Fry in hot oil until golden, drain on paper towels; serve hot.

"PIZZELLE"
MINIATURE PIZZAS

PIZZA DOUGH

TOMATO SAUCE, SEE RECIPES
IN THIS BOOK

VEGETABLE OIL

When your pizza dough is ready, roll it out and make lots of little disks. Press down the middle of each one with the heel of your hand, so they are more than about 0.5cm (¼ inch) thick and the edges are slightly raised. Fry them, two at a time in hot oil; use a ladle to pour a little hot oil on top of each

"pizzella" to help them rise, the center will remain concave.
When they are golden, remove and drain. Arrange them on a hot plate and scoop tomato sauce or any condiment of your choice into the middle and serve.

"SCAGLIUOZZI"
FRIED CORN MEAL

200 G/8 OZ CORN MEAL

VEGETABLE OIL

0.6 L/3 CUPS WATER

Pour the cornmeal into a pan filled with boiling salted water. Cook for 40 minutes, stirring continuously.
Turn the cooked corn meal onto your work table, flatten it and let it cool. Cut medium size rectangles and fry them in hot oil until crispy and golden.
Drain and serve hot.

EGGS

FINTA TRIPPA CON POMODORO
OMELET IN TOMATO SAUCE

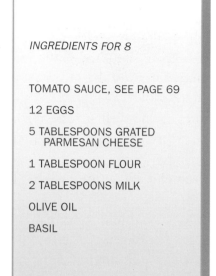

INGREDIENTS FOR 8

TOMATO SAUCE, SEE PAGE 69

12 EGGS

5 TABLESPOONS GRATED
    PARMESAN CHEESE

1 TABLESPOON FLOUR

2 TABLESPOONS MILK

OLIVE OIL

BASIL

Beat the eggs with the milk, a little parmesan cheese, flour, and a dash of salt and pepper.

Make thin little omelets in a pan. Roll up the omelets and cut them into strips that will resemble tripes. Prepare the tomato sauce according to the recipe on page 69. Put the strips into the tomato sauce and cook for just 5 minutes.

Garnish with a generous sprinkling of parmesan cheese and basil leaves.

FRITTATA DI CIPOLLE
ONION OMELET

INGREDIENTS FOR 8

12 EGGS

1.2 KG/2 ½ LB ONION

100 G/4 OZ GRATED
    PARMESAN AND PECORINO
    CHEESE

OLIVE OIL

PARSLEY, CHOPPED

Clean and slice the onions.

Brown in saucepan with a little water, a squiggle of olive oil and a pinch of salt. Start with a covered pan, then uncover it. Drain the onions and set aside to cool.

Combine the eggs, chopped parsley and grated cheeses in a large bowl, add a pinch of salt and a dash of pepper and beat together. Add the onions and keep on mixing. Coat a medium size pan with a little olive oil, pour in the egg and onion mixture. Cook over a low flame and turn the omelet a few times so that it cooks and browns evenly on both sides.

FRITTATA DI "FRIARIELLI"
TURNIP TOP OMELET

INGREDIENTS FOR 8

12 EGGS

1.5 KG/3 LB TURNIP GREENS

100 G/4 OZ GRATED PARMESAN AND PECORINO CHEESE

OLIVE OIL

1 CLOVE GARLIC

In a large bowl, combine the eggs, grated cheeses, a pinch of salt and a dash of pepper and beat well.

Cook the turnip greens briefly in boiling salted water, remove, and squeeze out the excess water. In a saucepan, sauté the garlic in a little olive oil until golden, then remove it. Add the greens, and cook covered until tender. Drain and let cool.

Then add them to the egg mixture and blend well. Grease a pan with a little oil and pour in the egg mixture, make sure to smooth it to an even thickness.

Cook over a low flame and turn the omelet a few times so that it cooks and browns evenly on both sides.

FRITTATA AL POMODORO
TOMATO OMELET

INGREDIENTS FOR 8

12 EGGS

700 G/1 $\frac{3}{4}$ LB FRESH TOMATOES

5 TABLESPOONS GRATED PARMESAN CHEESE

2 TABLESPOONS OLIVE OIL

1 ONION

Cut the tomatoes in medium size chunks, let them drain off the liquid. Slice the onion thinly and sauté in olive oil until tender, add the tomatoes, cook and stir frequently.

In a small bowl, combine the eggs, and parmesan cheese, salt, add a dash of pepper and beat well.

Add the cooked tomatoes to the egg and cheese mixture and stir until blended.

Pour the mixture into a large pan, turn the omelet at least twice so that it cooks evenly on both sides. When it starts to get golden, remove from the stove and serve hot.

FRITTATA DI SPAGHETTI IN BIANCO
SPAGHETTI OMELET

3 EGGS

400 G/1 LB SPAGHETTI

3 TABLESPOONS MILK

60 G/2 OZ GRATED PARMESAN CHEESE

50 G/2 OZ BUTTER

1 TABLESPOON OLIVE OIL

PARSLEY

Cook the spaghetti in boiling salted water until they are *al dente*, drain and dress with the parmesan cheese and butter, and add the lukewarm milk. Beat the eggs with chopped parsley and a dash of pepper, then pour the mixture over the spaghetti, use 2 forks to combine the ingredients.

Heat a little olive oil in a large pan, add the spaghetti and egg mixture and flatten it.

Cook over a low flame and turn the omelet a few times so that it cooks and browns evenly on both sides.

FRITTATA DI RICOTTA AL FORNO
BAKED RICOTTA OMELET

INGREDIENTS FOR 8

12 EGGS

750 G/ ³/₄ LB TOMATO SAUCE,
    SEE PAGE 69

100 G/4 OZ NEAPOLITAN
    SALAMI

350 G/13 OZ RICOTTA CHEESE

150 G/6 OZ MOZZARELLA
    CHEESE

3 TABLESPOONS FLOUR

3 TABLESPOONS MILK

4 TABLESPOONS GRATED
    PARMESAN CHEESE

In a large bowl, combine the eggs and dash each of salt and pepper, beat well, add the milk and generous dusting of flour, mix until evenly blended.

Heat a little oil in a pan, and put 2 tablespoons of the egg mixture to cook at a time, making many little omelets. Be sure to turn them so they cook evenly on both sides. When all the omelets are ready, put them on your work table.

In a bowl, combine the ricotta cheese, the mozzarella cut into little pieces, the salami, cut up and the grated parmesan cheese. Add the tomato sauce, stir until well blended.

Put a little of this mixture onto each omelet; roll up the omelets and press down the ends to keep the filling from seeping out.

Put tomato sauce in the bottom of an oven dish, arrange the rolled omelets side by side, top with more sauce and a sprinkling of parmesan cheese. Bake 200°C/390°F for just 15 minutes.

OMELETTE AL FIORDILATTE
MOZZARELLA OMELET

8 EGGS

150 G/6 OZ FRESH
    MOZZARELLA CHEESE

2 TABLESPOONS GRATED
    PARMESAN CHEESE

2 TABLESPOONS OLIVE OIL

BASIL

Cut the mozzarella into small cubes and set aside.

In a small bowl, combine the eggs, grated parmesan cheese, a pinch of salt and a dash of pepper, beat well. Heat a little olive oil in a pan, pour in the egg mixture and cook until the bottom begins to set. Put the mozzarella cubes and a little basil on top. Fold the omelet in half and continue cooking over a very low flame for a few minutes so that the mozzarella will melt. Slice before serving.

UOVA IN PURGATORIO
EGGS IN PURGATORY

INGREDIENTS FOR 8

12 EGGS

TOMATO SAUCE, SEE PAGE 69

BASIL

Make fresh tomato sauce according to the recipe on page 69. Break and separate the eggs, so that the yolk is in one half of the shell, the white in the other.

Pour the egg whites one, at a time, into the saucepan containing the tomato sauce and cook over a high flame until the whites set. Now carefully place a yolk over each cooked white, drench with boiling hot tomato sauce.

Serve immediately with fresh basil as garnish.

DESSERTS

BABÀ

FOR THE BABA:

350 G/13 OZ FLOUR

60 G/2 OZ SUGAR

3 EGGS

200 G/8 OZ BUTTER

30 G/1 OZ BREWER'S YEAST

1 GLASS MILK

FOR THE SYRUP:

100 G/4 OZ SUGAR

THE PEEL OF ONE LEMON

1 GLASS RUM

0.5 L/2 $^1/_2$ CUPS WATER

Dissolve the yeast in lukewarm milk and combine it with $^1/_3$ of the flour, blend until the dough is soft and smooth. Shape it into a loaf and let it rise until it doubles.

In the meantime beat the eggs, grease a tube pan with butter, and soften the rest of the butter.

Pour the flour on work table and combine all the ingredients with the risen loaf.

Knead thoroughly and delicately. Put the dough in the greased pan, filling it to $^1/_3$ of its capacity. Cover and let rise. When the dough reaches $^2/_3$ of the pan's capacity, bake in a moderate oven until it rises and is done inside (a knife or toothpick inserted in the middle should come out clean); raise the oven temperature to 190°C/375°F and continue baking until golden.

Remove the cake from the oven and let it cool in the pan; turn it out when it has cooled completely.

While it is baking, prepared the syrup. Boil the water with the sugar and the lemon peel, until it thickens.

Remove from the stove and set aside; when it has cooled a little, add the rum and stir well. Pour it over the cooled baba gradually until it is fully absorbed.

BIANCOMANGIARE
BLANCMANGE

120 G/5 OZ CORNSTARCH

200 G/8 OZ SUGAR

1 L MILK

ZEST OF ONE LEMON

In a saucepan, dissolve the cornstarch in milk and add the sugar and lemon zest.

Cook over a moderate flame, stirring constantly in the same direction, until the mixture thickens. Remove the lemon zest and pour the pudding into small, slightly moistened molds, refrigerate for several hours. Dip the molds into hot water and turn out the pudding. Serve with biscuits or small pastries.

CHIACCHIERE DI CARNEVALE
SWEET PASTRY FRITTERS FOR MARDI GRAS

400 G/1 LB FLOUR

80 G/3 OZ SUGAR

50 G/2 OZ BUTTER, MELTED

1 EGG + 2 YOLKS

CONFECTIONER'S SUGAR

3 TABLESPOONS EAU DE VIE

Put the flour on your work table in a mound, make a well in the middle and add the sugar, eggs a pinch of salt, the eau de vie and melted butter. Knead together well. Set aside for 30 minutes. Roll out the dough and cut it with into strips with a pastry cutting wheel. Tie a knot in each strip. Fry in hot oil, drain on paper towels and dust with confectioner's sugar.

GLASSA BIANCA
WHITE ICING

250 G/8 OZ CONFECTIONER'S
    SUGAR

BAKING SODA

6 TEASPOONS WATER

Combine the sugar with a pinch of baking soda and the water, boil in a small saucepan and monitor closely. After a few minutes test for doneness, take a drop of syrup between two fingers, if they do not stick together, the syrup is done.

Remove from the stove and pour into a bowl, stirring constantly until it becomes white and creamy.

Cover and store in a cool place.

PASTIERA

INGREDIENTS FOR 6

SHORT PASTRY, SEE PAGE 72

FOR THE CUSTARD

75 G/3 OZ FLOUR

3 EGG YOLKS

3 TABLESPOONS SUGAR

0.5 L/2 CUPS MILK

ZEST OF ONE LEMON

FOR THE FILLING:

200 G/8 OZ RICOTTA CHEESE

2 EGGS

120 G/5 OZ SUGAR

FLOWER ESSENCE LIQUEUR

80 G/3 OZ ASSORTED CANDIED
    FRUITS, CHOPPED

FOR THE WHEAT:

150 G/6 OZ MOISTENED
    CRACKED WHEAT

1 GLASS MILK

1 PAT BUTTER

1 SACHET VANILLA
    POWDER/ $^1/_2$ TEASPOON
    VANILLA EXTRACT

The day before you want bake the pastiera cook the cracked wheat in milk flavored with vanilla and butter for several hours over a low flame. The wheat will be done when the kernels are open and the content of the saucepan is creamy.

Prepare the short pastry according to the recipe on page 72 and set it aside.

Prepare the custard by gently combining all the ingredients and cooking briefly over a low flame, set aside to cool.

Beat the egg whites until stiff, and set aside.

In a large bowl, combine the ricotta cheese and sugar and mix thoroughly; gradually add the custard, stirring gently and the egg yolks, one at a time, stirring after each. When the mixture is well blended, add the cooled wheat, stirring all the time, as well as the chopped candied fruits, the flower essence liqueur and the stiffly beaten egg whites.

Roll out half the short pastry on a sheet of wax paper; butter a round, baking pan, 25 cm in diameter, 4 cm high, and turn the dough into it. Press the dough against the bottom and sides of the pan. Pour in the ricotta filling and smooth it evenly.

Roll out the rest of the dough on wax paper and cut into strips, 2 cm ($^3/_4$ inch) wide and lay them across the top of the pastiera forming a lattice.

Bake at 180°C/350°F for 1 hour, until the pastry is golden and the filling compact to a light touch.

Remove from the oven, and sprinkle with confectioner's sugar before serving.

PASTICCINI DI CREMA E AMARENE
CUSTARD AND WILD BLACK CHERRY PASTRIES

SHORT PASTRY, SEE PAGE 72

500 G/1 LB WILD BLACK
    CHERRY JAM

CONFECTIONER'S SUGAR

FOR THE CUSTARD

150 G/6 OZ FLOUR

6 EGG YOLKS

6 TABLESPOONS SUGAR

1 L MILK

ZEST OF ONE LEMON

Follow the instructions on the preceding page for the custard.

Prepare the short pastry according to the recipe on page 72. Roll out the dough on wax paper and cut disks, use half the dough to line molds. Put an even layer of custard in each and smooth it, top with a layer of wild black cherry jam and cover with another, smoothed layer of custard. Cover each mold with a disk of short pastry and press the edges to seal.

Bake in a hot oven for 40 minutes, until golden.

Remove and let cool. Turn out the pastries, dust with confectioner's and top with a teaspoon of wild black cherry jam.

SANGUINACCIO SENZA SANGUE
MOCK BLACK PUDDING

200 G/8 OZ BAKER'S CHOCOLATE

200 G/8 OZ PLAIN DRY COCOA

600 G/12 OZ SUGAR

50 G/2 OZ BUTTER, MELTED

70 G/3 OZ CORNSTARCH

1 LITER/1 QUART MILK

1 TEASPOON GROUND CINNAMON

1 SACHET VANILLA POWDER/
   $^1/_2$ TEASPOON VANILLA
   EXTRACT

CANDIED CITRON

In one bowl, combine the sugar, cinnamon and cocoa. In another bowl, dissolve the cornstarch in 1 cup of milk.

Pour the contents of both bowls into a saucepan, add the melted butter, the rest of the milk and the chocolate.

Bring to a boil and cook for 30 minutes stirring constantly until the cream thickens. Remove from stove, let cool, blend in the vanilla and the candied citron.

STRUFFOLI

400 G/17 OZ FLOUR

5 EGGS

1 TABLESPOON LARD

250 G/8 OZ GOLDEN HONEY

120 G/5 OZ SUGAR

PEANUT OIL

150 G/6 OZ/1 CUP CANDIED
   CITRUS PEEL, COCOZZATA,
   CHOPPED

ZEST OF 1 LEMON, GRATED

50 G/2 OZ NONPAREILS

VODKA

Pour the flour onto the work table in a mound, make a well in the center and add the eggs, sugar, lard, a pinch of salt, the grated lemon zest and a teaspoon of vodka.

Knead the dough and then it aside for 1 hour.

Take a fistful of dough and shape into sticks, about as thick as a finger; cut them into 1.5 cm ($^3/_4$ inch) long pieces and lay them out separately on a floured cloth.

Fry a few pieces of the dough at a time in hot oil; make sure they cook on the inside! Remove them as they are done, and put them on paper towels to drain.

Simmer the honey in a saucepan with the sugar and a little water until the syrup becomes golden.

Remove the saucepan from the stove, add the fried struffoli, half the chopped candied fruit and stir gently until the struffoli have absorbed the syrup. Pour the contents of the pan onto a serving dish and shape into a dome or circle. Decorate it with the "colored nonpareils" and the rest of the candied fruits.

SUSAMIELLI

80 G/3 OZ FLOUR

30 G/1 OZ SUGAR

40 G/1 OZ ALMONDS

80 G/3 OZ HONEY

PINCH OF CINNAMON

250 G/8 OZ CANDIED FRUIT

PINCH OF PEPPER

Boil the honey in a small saucepan for a few minutes. Place the flour on the work table in a mound, made a well in the center and add the finely chopped candied fruit, the whole almonds, sugar, spices and warm honey. First mix quickly with a spoon, then with your hands (when the honey has cooled sufficiently) so that all the ingredients blend with the flour. Roll out the dough to a thickness of 1.5 cm (³/₄ inch), cut round or oval pieces. Grease an oven sheet place the circles and ovals on it and bake in a moderate oven for 15 minutes.

RAFFIUOLI

100 G/4 OZ FLOUR

85 G/3 OZ SUGAR

ICING

2 EGGS

PINCH OF VANILLA POWDER

40 G/2 OZ APRICOT JAM

1 TEASPOON GRATED LEMON ZEST

Beat the egg yolks and sugar until light and creamy. Gradually pour in the flour, grated lemon zest and vanilla powder.

Beat the egg whites until stiff and gently fold into the yolk mixture. Put the mixture into a pastry bag and squeeze a 6 cm long strip onto a baking sheet, go back up in the opposite direction, and squeeze a second strip on top of the first taking care not to "break" it.

Continue squeezing out double strips. Make sure there is enough space between them because they tend to broaden and flatten. Bake in a moderate oven for 15 minutes. Remove and cool. In the meantime heat the apricot jam with 2 tablespoons of sugar and a small glass of water. Spread a thin layer of the softened jam on the pastries and then brush with icing.

To make the icing beat 3 egg whites with 150 g/6 oz granulated sugar.

Serve the raffiuoli well they are completely cooled.

ROCOCÒ

200 G/8 OZ FLOUR

200 G/8 OZ SUGAR

80 G/3 OZ ALMONDS

1 EGG

PINCH OF CINNAMON

60 G/2 OZ CANDIED CITRON AND ORANGE PEEL

GRATED ORANGE PEEL

Put the almonds in a pan and toast in a hot oven. Chop part of the almonds and combine with the sugar, candied fruits and the grated orange peel.

Put the flour on the work table in a mound, make a well in the middle and put the nut and fruit mixture into it, add a pinch of cinnamon. Add a little water and blend until the dough is reasonably stiff. Make 8 little sticks. about 1 cm ($^1/_2$ inch) thick and make circles; garnish with the remaining whole almonds.

Put the rococò on a greased oven sheet, brush with beaten egg yolk and bake in a medium-high oven for 10-15 minutes.

ZEPPOLE DI SAN GIUSEPPE

300 G/12 OZ FLOUR

50 G/2 OZ BUTTER

5 EGG YOLKS

2 EGG WHITES

2 CUPS WATER

Combine 2 cups water, a pinch of salt and the butter in a saucepan, when the butter is melted and the water starts to boil, add the flour and stir thoroughly. Cook over a low flame until the mixture comes away from the sides of the pan. Turn the mixture onto greased paper and let it cool. Add the egg yolks and the 2 whites and mix with your hands until air bubbles begin to form.

Let the dough rest for 30 minutes. Take a pastry syringe with a star-shaped tip. Grease a skimmer/, squeeze a circle of dough onto the skimmer and dip it into a pan of warm oil. The dough will come away from the skimmer as soon as touches the oil. When it puffs up, remove it and immediately put it into another pan with very hot oil and leave it there just until it gets golden. Remove and drain on paper towels. Repeat until you have used all the dough.

When the pastries are well-drained, fill the middle with a spoonful of custard (use the recipe on page 186) and top with 2 or 3 wild black cherries.